Abortion

OPPOSING VIEWPOINTS®

James D. Torr, *Book Editor*

Bruce Glassman, *Vice President*
Bonnie Szumski, *Publisher*
Helen Cothran, *Managing Editor*

OPPOSING VIEWPOINTS® SERIES

GREENHAVEN PRESS
An imprint of Thomson Gale, a part of The Thomson Corporation

THOMSON
★
GALE

Detroit • New York • San Francisco • San Diego • New Haven, Conn.
Waterville, Maine • London • Munich

OCT 2 8 2005

THOMSON

™

GALE

© 2006 Thomson Gale, a part of The Thomson Corporation.

Thomson and Star Logo are trademarks and Gale and Greenhaven Press are registered trademarks used herein under license.

For more information, contact
Greenhaven Press
27500 Drake Rd.
Farmington Hills, MI 48331-3535
Or you can visit our Internet site at http://www.gale.com

Cover credit: © Shawn Thew/EPA/Landov

LIBRARY OF CONGRESS CATALOGING-IN-PUBLICATION DATA
Abortion / James D. Torr, book editor.
p. cm. — (Opposing viewpoints)
Includes bibliographical references and index.
ISBN 0-7377-2921-X (lib. bdg. : alk. paper) —
ISBN 0-7377-2922-8 (pbk. : alk. paper)
1. Abortion—Moral and ethical aspects. 2. Abortion. I. Torr, James D., 1974– .
II. Opposing viewpoints series (Unnumbered)
HQ767.15.A23 2006
179.7'6—dc22   2005046396

Printed in the United States of America

"Congress shall make no law. . . abridging the freedom of speech, or of the press."

First Amendment to the U.S. Constitution

The basic foundation of our democracy is the First Amendment guarantee of freedom of expression. The Opposing Viewpoints Series is dedicated to the concept of this basic freedom and the idea that it is more important to practice it than to enshrine it.

Contents

Why Consider Opposing Viewpoints?

"The only way in which a human being can make some approach to knowing the whole of a subject is by hearing what can be said about it by persons of every variety of opinion and studying all modes in which it can be looked at by every character of mind. No wise man ever acquired his wisdom in any mode but this."

John Stuart Mill

In our media-intensive culture it is not difficult to find differing opinions. Thousands of newspapers and magazines and dozens of radio and television talk shows resound with differing points of view. The difficulty lies in deciding which opinion to agree with and which "experts" seem the most credible. The more inundated we become with differing opinions and claims, the more essential it is to hone critical reading and thinking skills to evaluate these ideas. Opposing Viewpoints books address this problem directly by presenting stimulating debates that can be used to enhance and teach these skills. The varied opinions contained in each book examine many different aspects of a single issue. While examining these conveniently edited opposing views, readers can develop critical thinking skills such as the ability to compare and contrast authors' credibility, facts, argumentation styles, use of persuasive techniques, and other stylistic tools. In short, the Opposing Viewpoints Series is an ideal way to attain the higher-level thinking and reading skills so essential in a culture of diverse and contradictory opinions.

In addition to providing a tool for critical thinking, Opposing Viewpoints books challenge readers to question their own strongly held opinions and assumptions. Most people form their opinions on the basis of upbringing, peer pressure, and personal, cultural, or professional bias. By reading carefully balanced opposing views, readers must directly confront new ideas as well as the opinions of those with whom they disagree. This is not to simplistically argue that everyone who reads opposing views will—or should—change his or her opinion. Instead, the series enhances readers' understanding of their own views by encouraging confrontation with opposing ideas. Careful examination of others' views can lead to the readers' understanding of the logical inconsistencies in their own opinions, perspective on why they hold an opinion, and the consideration of the possibility that their opinion requires further evaluation.

Evaluating Other Opinions

To ensure that this type of examination occurs, Opposing Viewpoints books present all types of opinions. Prominent spokespeople on different sides of each issue as well as well-known professionals from many disciplines challenge the reader. An additional goal of the series is to provide a forum for other, less known, or even unpopular viewpoints. The opinion of an ordinary person who has had to make the decision to cut off life support from a terminally ill relative, for example, may be just as valuable and provide just as much insight as a medical ethicist's professional opinion. The editors have two additional purposes in including these less known views. One, the editors encourage readers to respect others' opinions—even when not enhanced by professional credibility. It is only by reading or listening to and objectively evaluating others' ideas that one can determine whether they are worthy of consideration. Two, the inclusion of such viewpoints encourages the important critical thinking skill of objectively evaluating an author's credentials and bias. This evaluation will illuminate an author's reasons for taking a particular stance on an issue and will aid in readers' evaluation of the author's ideas.

It is our hope that these books will give readers a deeper understanding of the issues debated and an appreciation of the complexity of even seemingly simple issues when good and honest people disagree. This awareness is particularly important in a democratic society such as ours in which people enter into public debate to determine the common good. Those with whom one disagrees should not be regarded as enemies but rather as people whose views deserve careful examination and may shed light on one's own.

Thomas Jefferson once said that "difference of opinion leads to inquiry, and inquiry to truth." Jefferson, a broadly educated man, argued that "if a nation expects to be ignorant and free . . . it expects what never was and never will be." As individuals and as a nation, it is imperative that we consider the opinions of others and examine them with skill and discernment. The Opposing Viewpoints Series is intended to help readers achieve this goal.

David L. Bender and Bruno Leone,
Founders

Greenhaven Press anthologies primarily consist of previously published material taken from a variety of sources, including periodicals, books, scholarly journals, newspapers, government documents, and position papers from private and public organizations. These original sources are often edited for length and to ensure their accessibility for a young adult audience. The anthology editors also change the original titles of these works in order to clearly present the main thesis of each viewpoint and to explicitly indicate the opinion presented in the viewpoint. These alterations are made in consideration of both the reading and comprehension levels of a young adult audience. Every effort is made to ensure that Greenhaven Press accurately reflects the original intent of the authors included in this anthology.

Introduction

"Roe v. Wade may have liberated many women; yet it has also trapped America in an irresolvable clash of absolutes."

—The Economist

Since 1973, when it became legal nationwide, abortion has been one of the most persistently controversial issues in American politics and culture. As *Time* journalist Roger Simon writes, for many Americans legal abortion "represents an American holocaust, a mass murder of the unborn" while for many others it "represents the ability of women to control their own bodies and destinies and maintain a right of privacy free from the intervention of government." Abortion is intensely controversial because it involves several interwoven issues: the question of when life begins and the moral status of the embryo or fetus; the moral status of the pregnant woman and her right to reproductive autonomy; and the role of government in regulating the procedure.

Controversy over abortion existed prior to 1973. In the early 1960s most states prohibited abortion except in cases when the woman's life would be endangered if she carried the pregnancy to term. By the late 1960s several states had also made exceptions for cases of rape, incest, or when the fetus had a severe defect. Spurred by the growing abortion rights movement, in 1972 four states allowed all abortions that were judged necessary by a woman and her doctor.

In 1973 the Supreme Court issued its landmark ruling in *Roe v. Wade*. The case centered around a Texas law that prohibited abortion except in cases where it was necessary to save the life of the mother. The Court found that the Fourteenth Amendment's right of personal privacy "is broad enough to encompass a woman's decision whether or not to terminate her pregnancy." The Court also ruled that the state had a limited interest in protecting maternal health and the potential life of the fetus, but that this only became a "compelling interest" after viability—the point at which the fetus can survive outside the womb. Many issues surrounding abortion were not addressed in *Roe*, but its main effect was clear: State laws banning first-trimester abortions were unconstitutional.

As *Congressional Digest* notes, "Rather than settling the issue of a woman's right to terminate her pregnancy, the U.S. Supreme Court's ruling in 1973 kindled heated debate." In many states anti-abortion legislators continued to push for restrictive abortion laws, with the courts determining which laws were constitutional under *Roe* and which were not. In a variety of rulings, the Supreme Court refined its position on abortion rights. The most important of these rulings came in the 1992 case of *Planned Parenthood v. Casey*, in which the Court moved away from the viability standard set in *Roe* and instead expanded states' authority to regulate abortion so long as such regulations do not place an "undue burden" on a woman's ability to have an abortion.

Anti-abortion legislators continue to test the bounds of this new standard. Since the 1990s, bans on "dilation and extraction" or "D&X" abortions have been the most controversial type of abortion law. In this rarely performed abortion procedure, the body of the fetus is extracted from the uterus and vagina, then the fetus is killed by extracting the contents of its skull. The skull is then collapsed and the intact fetus is removed. Abortion opponents have labeled the D&X procedure "partial-birth abortion"; pro-choice groups object to this label on the grounds that it is a nonmedical term that connotes infanticide.

State bans on partial-birth abortion have repeatedly been struck down by the Supreme Court as unconstitutional. Despite this, in November 2003 President George W. Bush signed into law the first federal partial-birth abortion ban. Pro-choice groups have vowed to fight the law: "This bill marks a concerted effort to set back decades of progress in achieving reproductive freedom," said Planned Parenthood president Gloria Feldt. The Partial Birth Abortion Ban Act marks the first-ever federal law making an abortion procedure a crime, and opponents on both sides of the debate view its passage as evidence that the anti-abortion movement is as strong as ever. Dave Andrusko, editor of *National Right to Life News*, contends that "in years to come historians will look back at the Partial Birth Abortion Ban Act of 2003 and view it as the turning point."

Abortion rights advocates worry that a different "turning point" may be near—that, if given the chance, President George W. Bush will appoint an antiabortion judge to the Supreme Court. With a conservative majority on the Court, these analysts worry that *Roe v. Wade* might be overturned. "Anti-choice forces are counting on new appointments to the Supreme Court in the next few years to totally overturn *Roe*," warns the Center for Reproductive Rights.

There is some evidence that support for *Roe* and abortion rights in general is on the wane. In a 2002 Gallup poll, only 24 percent of Americans said that abortion should be legal in all cases, down from 34 percent in 1992. And in 2002 abortion rates reached their lowest levels since 1974. Andrusko predicts that "the American people are close to 'catching' the pro-life vision."

On the other hand, legal abortion has been the law of the land for more than three decades, and those who have grown up with abortion rights may not want to lose them. While abortion rates are declining, the procedure is still common: About 25 percent of all pregnancies in the United States end in abortion, and an estimated 35 percent of all U.S. women will have an abortion in their lifetimes. According to the opinion research organization Public Agenda, 66 percent of Americans believe that abortion should be legal through the first three months of pregnancy. If *Roe* were overturned, there could be an enormous political backlash.

The authors in *Opposing Viewpoints: Abortion* debate *Roe*, the ethics of abortion, and related issues in the following chapters: Is Abortion Immoral? Does Abortion Benefit Women? Should Abortion Rights Be Restricted? Do Genetic Technologies Destroy Human Life? Whatever the future of *Roe v. Wade*, abortion is bound to remain one of America's most divisive issues. As the *Economist* predicts—assuming that it will not be overturned—"The fortieth anniversary of *Roe v. Wade* will be just as acrimonious as the thirtieth."

CHAPTER 1

Is Abortion Immoral?

Chapter Preface

One reason that the abortion debate is so contentious is that advocates on each side of the controversy often frame the issue in different ways. Opponents of abortion tend to speak in terms of life and death while defenders of abortion tend to focus on individual rights. Each side feels that the other is failing to grasp the salient points of the debate.

When it comes to the ethics of abortion, opponents of abortion tend to focus on the value of human life and the question of when it begins. For example, the conservative advocacy organization Focus on the Family begins its statement on abortion with, "All human life is of inestimable worth and significance, including the preborn." When opponents of abortion talk about rights, they usually speak of fetus's "right to life," hence the term *pro-life*.

Defenders of abortion refer to themselves as "pro-choice," and to opponents as "anti-choice" since they view the abortion issue in terms of a woman's right to make decisions about her body. The abortion rights organization NARAL Pro-Choice America claims that it is "the only organization with a proven history and expertise to combat an aggressive anti-choice movement intent on taking away our rights and freedoms." For most pro-choice advocates, the most important moral question in the abortion debate is not when life begins or whether the fetus has a "right to life," but whether a woman's right to control her body should ever be taken away.

Of course, advocates on each side of the issue are aware of the other side's point of view. Pro-choice advocates will sometimes address pro-lifers' concerns about abortion as killing, and pro-lifers will sometimes discuss their position in terms of women's rights. The authors in the following chapter debate the morality of abortion, presenting their arguments using these by-now familiar terms.

"The act of abortion is an intrinsically evil act."

Abortion Is Immoral

William P. Saunders

William P. Saunders is pastor of Our Lady of Hope Parish in Potomac Falls, Virginia, and former dean of the Notre Dame Graduate School of Christendom College. The following viewpoint is excerpted from an editorial that Saunders wrote for the *Catholic Herald*, the official newspaper of the Roman Catholic Diocese of Arlington, Virginia. In it, he maintains that abortion involves the deliberate destruction of human life and is therefore murder. Saunders argues that there is only one morally correct decision that can be made concerning abortion, and that is to preserve the life of the unborn.

As you read, consider the following questions:
1. What first-century church document does Saunders cite as prohibiting abortion?
2. What historical evils does Saunders compare abortion to?
3. What biblical commandment does abortion violate, according to the author?

William P. Saunders, "Against Abortion, but Pro-Choice?" *Catholic Herald*, January 23, 2003. Copyright © 2003 by the Arlington Catholic Herald. All rights reserved. Reproduced by permission.

Sometimes I have met Catholics—especially where I work— who say, "I am personally against abortion, but I am pro-choice." To me, that makes no sense, but how can I argue with them?—A reader in Alexandria

The pro-abortion movement has made great gains using the "pro-choice" label. First, the "pro-choice" label numbs our moral sensitivity because it masks that anyone really is for abortion, ignores scientific and medical evidence and diverts attention from the act itself. Secondly, the idea of being "pro-choice" seems to appeal to Americans who cherish freedom and the idea of being free to choose rather than being forced to do anything.

Scientific Evidence

In arguing against this "pro-choice" position, one must first focus on the heart of the choice—a child. Proceeding from a purely scientific approach, we know that when conception occurs, a new and unique human being is created. The DNA genetic code attests to this uniqueness. (Why else has DNA coding become so important in identifying criminals?) Moreover, from that moment of conception, the child continues to develop and to grow; the child is born, matures to adolescence and then adulthood and eventually dies. Note though that this is all the same person who was conceived: all that has been added is nourishment, time and hopefully a lot of love. Therefore, our Church teaches, "From the time that the ovum is fertilized, a life is begun which is neither that of the father nor of the mother; it is rather the life of a new human being with his own growth. It would never be made human if it were not human already" (*Declaration on Procured Abortion*, no. 12, 1974).

For further information, please check the November 11, 2002, issue of *Time* entitled, "Inside the Womb: An Amazing Look at How We All Began; The Latest Science on How Healthy Babies Are Born." Also the video and book under the same title, *The Miracle of Life*, are also excellent resources.

Interestingly, this past Fall [2002], General Electric had a commercial showing the new technology/photography they developed enabling doctors to see clearly and in color the baby developing inside the womb of the mother. This new technology far surpasses that of ultrasound. When I first saw the commercial, I said, "Seeing this, how could anyone be for abortion?" The commercial had an impact: Planned Parenthood and the Abortion Rights Action League lobbied General Electric so much that they removed the commercial from television.

Catholic Doctrine

Moving beyond science to the level of faith, we also believe that almighty God creates and infuses a unique and immortal soul into that body. This soul—our spiritual principle—is what gives each person that identity of being made in God's image and likeness. Even if there were some doubt that God infused the soul at conception or some doubt that the conceived child were truly a person, "it is objectively a grave sin to dare to risk murder. The one who will be a man is already one" (*Declaration*, no. 13).

We find in Sacred Scripture testimony to the sanctity of life in the womb: The Lord said to the mother of Sampson, "As for the son you will conceive and bear, no razor shall touch his head, for this boy is to be consecrated to God from the womb!" (Jgs 13:5). Job said, "Did not he who made me in the womb make him? Did not the same One fashion us before our birth?" (Jb 31:15). In Psalm 139:13, we pray, "Truly you have formed my inmost being; you knit me in my mother's womb." The Lord spoke to Jeremiah, "Before I formed you in the womb I knew you, before you were born I dedicated you, a prophet to the nations I appointed you" (Jer 1:5).

For Christians the sanctity of life in the womb and the belief that this truly is a person is further corroborated by the incarnation: Mary conceived by the power of the Holy Spirit, and Jesus Christ true God entered this world becoming also true man. Even though Jesus was still in the womb of His blessed mother, St. Elizabeth and St. John the Baptist, also in the womb, rejoiced at the presence of the Lord. Would anyone dare suggest Jesus was not a person in the womb of His mother? Little wonder in the *Didache* (*The Teachings of the Twelve Apostles*)—the first manual of doctrine, liturgical laws, and morals written about the year A.D. 80—we find the moral prohibition, "You shall not kill by abortion the fruit of the

Wright. © 2004 by Tribune Media Services. Reproduced by permission of the illustrator.

womb and you shall not murder the infant already born."

Given that the heart of the choice involves a unique, human person, the choice of action becomes clear: to preserve and safeguard the life of this person in the womb or to destroy it. Since this is a person, the latter choice does not involve simply a termination of a pregnancy or the removal of a fetus; rather, the latter choice involves a direct killing of an innocent person, a deliberate murder. Therefore, the act of abortion is an intrinsically evil act. The Second Vatican Council asserted, "Life must be protected with the utmost care from the moment of conception: abortion and infanticide are abominable crimes" (*Gaudium et Spes*, no. 51).

No Right to Choose Evil

We do not have the right to choose evil, no matter what the circumstances are or even if some sort of "good" may arise. To purposefully choose to do evil is an affront to God Himself, in whose image and likeness we are made. In the "prochoice position," one is not choosing between two good actions; instead, one is turning a blind eye to the objectively evil action of abortion and pretending that it is on the same moral standing as protecting the child in the womb. To say one is "pro-choice" in this matter is no different than saying one is "pro-choice" for apartheid, Nazi concentration camps, or Jim Crow segregation laws—"I am personally against it, but everybody should choose." Of course, the person who does not get to choose in any of these cases is the one society has deemed dispensable, disposable and unworthy of life.

Pope John Paul II stated, "Anyone can see that the alternative here is only apparent. It is not possible to speak of the right to choose when a clear moral evil is involved, when what is at stake is the commandment, 'Do not kill.'" (*Crossing the Threshold of Hope*, p. 205). Christians must continue to defend the sanctity of human life in the face of this insidious prochoice argument. To be "pro-life" is not to impose one's values on another; rather, to be "pro-life" is to uphold the truth of God and the dignity of every human being, born or unborn.

In those difficult, tragic situations—rape and incest (which result in conception at best 2% of the time depending upon which set of statistics one looks at), a young teenage pregnant mother, or a deformed or handicapped child—we must remember the child is still an innocent human being who through no fault of his own was conceived. Here sharing in the cross of our Lord becomes a reality without question. In these cases, we as members of the Church must support both the mother and the child through our prayers and by opening our hearts, homes and wallets to their needs. We must make the sacrifice to preserve human life.

In Fall, 2001, Bishop Loverde issued a letter to mark Respect Life Sunday in which he taught, "To be a faithful and serious Catholic necessarily means that one is pro-life and not pro-choice. To be pro-choice essentially means supporting the right of a woman to terminate the life of her baby, either preborn or partially born. No Catholic can claim to be a faithful and serious member of the Church while advocating for or actively supporting direct attacks on innocent human life. Moreover, protecting human life from conception until natural death is more than a Catholic issue. It is an issue of fundamental morality, rooted in both the natural and divine law."

"A woman deciding whether to continue a pregnancy stands on moral ground. She is entitled to make her decision."

Abortion Is Not Immoral

Caitlin Borgmann and Catherine Weiss

Caitlin Borgmann is state strategies coordinator, and Catherine Weiss is director, of the American Civil Liberties Union Reproductive Freedom Project. In the following viewpoint they argue that since the legalization of abortion in 1973, the public has become complacent about abortion rights. People should be reminded of the ethical arguments that led to the legalization of abortion in the first place, they assert. Borgmann and Weiss maintain that the decision of whether or not to continue a pregnancy rests solely with the pregnant woman. They believe that laws against abortion prohibit women from making decisions about their own bodies, a violation of their human rights. Moreover, they maintain that such laws subjugate women and harm families by forcing women to bring unwanted children into the world.

As you read, consider the following questions:

1. How do antichoice leaders view women, in the authors' opinion?
2. How do laws against abortion undermine women's
 * equality, in the authors' view?
3. In what way are abortion rights pro-child, according to Borgmann and Weiss?

Caitlin Borgmann and Catherine Weiss, "Beyond Apocalypse and Apology: A Moral Defense of Abortion," *Perspectives on Sexual and Reproductive Health*, vol. 35, January/February 2003. Copyright © 2003 by The Alan Guttmacher Institute. Reproduced by permission.

The movement to preserve and advance reproductive freedom is suffering the consequences of a great victory. The establishment of the constitutional right to abortion in *Roe v. Wade* was a monumental step that changed the lives of American women. Girls grow up today under the mantle of *Roe*, never having known a world in which illegal, unsafe, degrading and sometimes fatal abortions were the norm. That is a cause for celebration. . . . It is also, however, a cause of complacency. Movements typically subside after winning major legal or political battles, and ours has not escaped this cycle.

Complacency corrodes all freedoms. It is particularly dangerous to reproductive freedom because our opponents are single-minded and fervent to the point of fanaticism. Their crusade has fueled three decades of incremental restrictions that make it risky or burdensome to get an abortion and, for some women, block access altogether. Understandably, the prochoice movement has grown frustrated with the unending onslaught, and the public, numb. The movement's responses to this conundrum have varied over time and among its many spokespersons. Yet, two recurring approaches—to jolt the public by forecasting *Roe*'s reversal and to court reluctant supporters by steering wide of abortion altogether—are problematic. We need to recapture at least some of the moral urgency that led to *Roe*, and we must meet the assaults head-on. . . .

Defending Abortion, Defending Women

To defend abortion with confidence, we must first recognize that institutional opposition to the right is part of a broader campaign to undermine women's autonomy and equality. Antichoice leaders see sexuality (especially women's) divorced from procreation as shameful, women as inadequate to make weighty moral decisions and forced childbearing as appropriate punishment for sexual irresponsibility. They approve of requiring women to pay out of pocket for contraception, while ensuring that insurance plans cover men's access to Viagra; reducing sexuality education to a "just say no" mantra and consigning those teenagers who say yes to the deadly risks of unprotected sex; and denying poor women the means to obtain abortions, yet refusing to help them provide adequate food, shelter and education for the children they bear. Abortion is only one piece of the puzzle.

When this puzzle is assembled, the image that emerges is of a woman subjugated, not a fetus saved. For example, it is illuminating that "right-to-life" leaders generally tolerate abortion in cases of rape or incest. The fetus conceived by rape is biologically and morally indistinguishable from the fetus conceived by voluntary intercourse. But in the view of our opponents, the rape victim is innocent while the woman who chooses to have sex is tainted. For them, it is the woman's innocence or guilt that determines whether she should be allowed to have an abortion or forced to bear a child.

Abortion Is a Human Right

Women have the right to decide whether or not to bring a pregnancy to term.

- The *right to physical integrity* ensures freedom from unwanted invasions of one's body. When a pregnancy is unwanted, its continuation can take a heavy toll on a woman's physical and emotional well-being. A woman's right to physical integrity entitles her to decide whether or not she will carry a pregnancy to term.

- A woman's *right to determine the number and spacing of her children* requires governments to make abortion services legal, safe, and accessible to all women. Women are entitled to have access to all safe, effective means of controlling their family size, including abortion. . . .

- Decisions one makes about one's body, particularly one's reproductive capacity, lie squarely in the domain of private decision-making. A woman's *right to privacy*, therefore, entitles her to decide whether or not to undergo an abortion without government interference. Only a pregnant woman knows whether she is ready to have a child, and governments can play no role in influencing that decision.

Center for Reproductive Rights, "Safe and Legal Abortion Is a Woman's Human Right," www.crlp.org, March 2000.

The impulse to punish women rather than to help children is equally evident in the polities of antichoice states with regard to children already born. If the motivation behind abortion restrictions were really the love of babies, antichoice states should have child-friendly laws. Yet the opposite is so. A comprehensive review of the abortion and child welfare policies in the 50 states demonstrates that the states with the most restrictive abortion laws also spend the least to facilitate adoption, to provide subsistence to poor children and to educate children in general. The study concludes, "Pro-life states are less likely than pro-choice states to provide adequate care to poor and needy children. Their concern for the weak and vulnerable appears to stop at birth." The seemingly contradictory coexistence of "pro-life" laws and antichild polities is explained, in significant part, by opposition to women's changing roles in society: The more hostile statewide public opinion is toward women's equality and the lower women's income is relative to men's, the more likely the state is both to restrict abortion and to impoverish children.

In contrast, our position is prowoman, profamily, prochild and prochoice. This is a moral debate we must have and can win. Such a debate can move doubters to become moral defenders of a woman's decision to have an abortion. Even those who remain personally opposed to abortion may come to support each woman's right to make the decision in accordance with her own conscience, commitments and beliefs. What follows are some of the best reasons to support abortion rights.

Autonomy

A woman deciding whether to continue a pregnancy stands on moral ground. She is entitled to make her decision, and she must live with the consequences. No one else—and certainly not the government—should decide whether she will use her body to bring new life into the world. The decision is too intimate and too important to be taken from her.

In everyday life, men and women make decisions that affect the life and death of existing people. They decide whether to join the army; whether to donate blood, a kidney or bone marrow to a child; whether to give money to Save the Children instead of buying a new sweater, whether to decline a lifesaving blood transfusion; whether to drive a small fort on wheels that may protect its passengers in a crash but often kills those in less-substantial vehicles. Few question adults' autonomy to make these decisions, although some may criticize the individual choice made.

Yet, our opponents want a different standard to govern women's decisions about abortion. They portray women who demand the right to make this decision as selfish and immoral, although even many "prolifers" place fetuses on a lower moral plane than existing people (hence their tolerance of abortion in cases of rape and incest, among other inconsistencies). In response, we must staunchly defend women's ability and right to be moral actors, especially when they are making decisions about reproduction.

Equality

Without the right of reproductive choice, women cannot participate equally in the nation's social, political and economic life. Their freedom to decide whether and when to have children opens doors that would otherwise be closed. They may learn to be electricians, librarians, roofers, teachers or triathletes; care for their young children or aging parents; start and finish college; wait until they are financially and emotionally prepared to support a child; keep a steady job; marry if and when they want to.

Women still do the bulk of the work of raising children and caring for extended families. Whether they experience this work as a privilege, a necessity, a burden or all three, increasing their control over the scope and timing of these responsibilities can only help them to secure a more equal footing on whatever paths they travel. In fact, in countries throughout the world, women's desire and ability to limit the number of children they have go hand in hand with their educational advancement and economic independence.

Body Integrity

Women should have control over their own bodies. In virtually all other contexts, the law treats a person's body as inviolable. Prisoners are denied many of their most important personal liberties, yet are protected from unreasonable invasions of their bodies (such as routine body cavity searches). Similarly, the state cannot require a crime victim to undergo an operation to recover evidence (such as a bullet), even if that evidence would help to convict a murder suspect. And no law can force an unwilling parent to undergo bodily invasions far less risky than pregnancy (such as donating bone marrow) to save a living child. [According to constitutional scholar Laurence H. Tribe,] "It is difficult to imagine a clearer case of bodily intrusion" than for the government to demand that a woman continue a pregnancy and go through childbirth against her will.

Wantedness and Women's Health

The decision to have a child—even more than the decision to have an abortion—carries profound moral implications. Unless a woman is willing to bear a child and give it up for adoption, she should have children when she feels she can welcome them. A mother's freedom to decide whether and when to have an additional child contributes immeasurably to the welfare of the children she already has, as well as any yet to be born. A teenager's decision to delay having a child until a time when she can provide adequate financial and emotional support increases the probability that when she does decide to have a family, it will be healthy and stable. Indeed, many women who decide not to have a child at a particular time do so out of reverence for children.

Finally, the right to abortion promotes personal and public health. We know that criminal bans do not stop women from seeking abortions. The desperate measures women in pre-*Roe* days felt driven to take to terminate their unwanted pregnancies are testament to how untenable the prospect of childbearing can be. Access to safe, legal abortion ensures that women will not be maimed or killed when they decide they cannot continue a pregnancy. Similarly, access to safe abortion ensures that women can terminate pregnancies that endanger their health. A pregnant woman with a heart condition, uncontrolled hypertension, diabetes or one of a host of other problems must have all medically accepted options open to her. She, her loved ones and her doctor must be able to respond to shifting and serious health risks without having to consult a lawyer.

Abortion Rights Are Moral Rights

These reasons to support abortion rights are not new. All of them predate *Roe v. Wade*, some by centuries. Yet, as *Roe* turns

30 [in 2003] and continues its embattled advance toward middle age, these reasons are as pressing as ever. We state them in different ways to appeal to different audiences at different times, but all provide a basis for persuading people to stand behind abortion rights, both for themselves and for others.

However persuasive we are, of course, a groundswell to defend the right to abortion may not rise up until enough people feel so personally threatened that they take action. Nevertheless, if we are clear, straightforward and unabashed about why we advocate for reproductive freedom, and realistic about the threats we face, we may rebuild public support, even if this support does not instantly translate into activism. Maintaining and reinforcing this support can, in turn, ready the public for a call to action. Thus, we preserve the best hope not only for mobilizing in a crisis, but also for targeted organizing against the disparate restrictions that are building into a barrier too high for many to cross.

| *"Life begins the moment a female egg is fertilized."*

Life Begins at Conception

Jon Dougherty

Jon Dougherty is a columnist for WorldNetDaily.com, a conservative Internet news site. In the following viewpoint Dougherty rejects the idea that abortion is justified because life does not begin until birth or, alternatively, until viability (the point at which the fetus can survive outside the womb). He contends that all abortion is murder because life begins at conception, when the male sperm and female egg combine. In his view those who argue that life begins at birth or in the second or third trimester are trying to fool themselves and others into condoning an immoral act.

As you read, consider the following questions:
1. What is the most common hypocrisy among supporters of abortion, in Dougherty's opinion?
2. When do human beings become viable, in Dougherty's view?
3. What three developmental stages does the author identify?

At this point in the "debate" over abortion, it is patently obvious that any justification given by pro-abortion advocates to continue our society's practice of butchering its young is neither valid nor sensible.

Worse, our nation has all but lost any claims we could have ever made on "compassion" because we have allowed lies, innuendo and insanity to circumscribe the parameters of this so-called debate. Such tactics have cheapened life so much that now we're to the point where millions of us are no longer capable of seeing the truth for the blood on our hands.

Perhaps the most egregious and common hypocrisy is the justification that abortion is okay because life doesn't "begin" until a human being is actually born—yet no self-respecting abortion advocate who spews this robotically-rehearsed and overused phrase can explain the miracle of life that scientists, doctors and parents have known for eons: Life begins at *conception*, not birth. Birth is simply one stage of ongoing human development.

The "Not Viable Life" Excuse

"Ho, ho," you laugh. "That Dougherty is clueless. 'Life' isn't 'life' until it's *viable* life; which means, when you're born, fully developed." To suppose this is true would be akin to the claim that death isn't death until we say it's death.

Life is as real and as tangible as death; consequently, we humans are "viable" the moment we are created in the womb. Barring death by natural causes, everyone has the potential to eventually become a senior citizen someday—as long as they aren't butchered before birth. In fact, some have said we begin to die the moment we are conceived because our lives always reach that inevitable conclusion.

The "not viable life" excuse doesn't hold up because, if all life is not "viable" life, then what is the purpose of having an abortion? If these human beings weren't viable and would not—if left unmolested—mature into "born" children and adults, then the abortion would be unnecessary to begin with.

Also—and this is key—we humans are never "fully-developed." We're not born "complete"; we grow, change, mature and age constantly, which means we're always "developing," and we develop through the first nine months of our lives attached to a "host"—our mothers.

So, the fact that the first nine months of our developmental life is *in utero* is of no consequence to our overall lifespan; it is just the first stage. There are many developmental stages —early, middle and late.

Asay. © by Charles Asay. Reproduced by permission.

But life has to begin somewhere. We don't go from "nothing" to adulthood.

Denying the Truth

Denying the fact that life begins the moment a female egg is fertilized is sheer lunacy—or, worse, intentionally misleading. It is simply a matter of choice that millions of Americans have decided to believe that life only begins when they say it does—at the moment of birth, or in the second trimester of pregnancy, or some other arbitrary guideline.

It begins when it *begins*—at the moment a human being is biologically "under construction."

Passing laws or writing constitutional mandates from the bench of the Supreme Court cannot change this fact. Indeed, it has not changed this fact; only our perception of the fact has changed, largely for reasons of personal convenience.

It is patently arrogant that we, as adults, get to decide for the most vulnerable of our society—our unborn children, who cannot speak for themselves—who lives and who dies. Or, if you prefer, who gets to experience further "development" and who doesn't.

If we intentionally end any stage of a human life in development, we are committing an act of murder, as it has been defined by our society from its humble beginnings.

Any attempt to convince ourselves otherwise is little more than a mental joust with reality and an injustice to our unborn that we can never excuse away, try as we may.

> *"A child cannot acquire any rights until it is born."*

Abortion Rights Are Pro-Life

Leonard Peikoff

Leonard Peikoff is founder of the Ayn Rand Institute, which promotes individual rights. In the following viewpoint Peikoff contends that embryos in the first trimester of pregnancy are not persons and therefore have no right to life. He grants that embryos are potential persons but claims that individual rights pertain only to actual, living persons. He concludes that the right of a woman to control her body should be recognized while the supposed rights of an embryo should not since the embryo is a clump of tissue and not an actual person.

As you read, consider the following questions:

1. What essential issue do anti-abortionists ignore, in Peikoff's opinion?
2. What reasons does the author list for why a woman might legitimately choose to have an abortion?
3. Why is the anti-abortionists' claim to being pro-life a "Big Lie," in the author's view?

Thirty years after *Roe v. Wade*, no one defends the right to abortion in fundamental moral terms, which is why the pro-abortion rights forces are on the defensive.

Abortion-rights advocates should not cede the terms "pro-life" and "right to life" to the anti-abortionists. It is a woman's right to her life that gives her the right to terminate her pregnancy.

Nor should abortion-rights advocates keep hiding behind the phrase "a woman's right to choose." Does she have the right to choose murder? That's what abortion would be, if the fetus were a person.

The status of the embryo in the first trimester is the basic issue that cannot be sidestepped. The embryo is clearly pre-human; only the mystical notions of religious dogma treat this clump of cells as constituting a person.

We must not confuse potentiality with actuality. An embryo is a potential human being. It can, granted the woman's choice, develop into an infant. But what it actually is during the first trimester is a mass of relatively undifferentiated cells that exist as a part of a woman's body. If we consider what it is rather than what it might become, we must acknowledge that the embryo under three months is something far more primitive than a frog or a fish. To compare it to an infant is ludicrous.

If we are to accept the equation of the potential with the actual and call the embryo an "unborn child," we could, with equal logic, call any adult an "undead corpse" and bury him alive or vivisect him for the instruction of medical students.

That tiny growth, that mass of protoplasm, exists as a part of a woman's body. It is not an independently existing, biologically formed organism, let alone a person. That which lives within the body of another can claim no right against its host. Rights belong only to individuals, not to collectives or to parts of an individual.

("Independent" does not mean self-supporting—a child who depends on its parents for food, shelter and clothing, has rights because it is an actual, separate human being.)

"Rights," in Ayn Rand's words, "do not pertain to a potential, only to an actual being. A child cannot acquire any rights until it is born."

It is only on this base that we can support the woman's political right to do what she chooses in this issue. No other person—not even her husband—has the right to dictate what she may do with her own body. That is a fundamental principle of freedom.

A Biblical View of When Life Begins

God never condemned nor condoned legal abortion in the bible. Given that God spoke to many other important issues—i.e., marriage and divorce, it's very telling that God didn't speak directly and in no uncertain terms to the issue of legal abortion, isn't it?

God recognized the official beginning of human life as being at birth. Genesis 2:7, "God breathed into his nostrils the breath of life and man became a living soul."

While the process God used to create Adam and Eve and a baby born today are very different—and with good reason—Adam and Eve being created as the mother and father of all mankind—Adam and Eve and a baby born today do share a common bond in the culmination of their creative processes.

They breathe the breath of life through the nostrils.

By God's own desire and design human beings born today don't breathe the breath of life through their nostrils until they're born.

Neither God nor Life and Liberty for Women has ever argued that the fetus isn't alive in the womb, but that fact doesn't speak to the official recognition by God of the beginning of life, that is at birth.

Peggy Loonan, "God, the Bible, and Abortion," www.lifeandlibertyfor women.org, 2003.

There are many legitimate reasons why a rational woman might have an abortion—accidental pregnancy, rape, birth defects, danger to her health. The issue here is the proper role for government. If a pregnant woman acts wantonly or capriciously, then she should be condemned morally—but not treated as a murderer.

If someone capriciously puts to death his cat or dog, that can well be reprehensible, even immoral, but it is not the province of the state to interfere. The same is true of an abortion which puts to death a far less-developed growth in a woman's body.

If anti-abortionists object that an embryo has the genetic equipment of a human being, remember: so does every cell in the human body.

Abortions are private affairs and often involve painfully difficult decisions with life-long consequences. But, tragically, the lives of the parents are completely ignored by the anti-abortionists. Yet that is the essential issue. In any conflict it's the actual, living persons who count, not the mere potential of the embryo.

Being a parent is a profound responsibility—financial, psychological, moral—across decades. Raising a child demands time, effort, thought and money. It's a full-time job for the first three years, consuming thousands of hours after that—as caretaker, supervisor, educator and mentor. To a woman who does not want it, this is a death sentence.

The anti-abortionists' attitude, however, is: "The actual life of the parents be damned! Give up your life, liberty, property and the pursuit of your own happiness."

Sentencing a woman to sacrifice her life to an embryo is not upholding the "right to life."

The anti-abortionists' claim to being "pro-life" is a classic Big Lie. You cannot be in favor of life and yet demand the sacrifice of an actual, living individual to a clump of tissue.

Anti-abortionists are not lovers of life—lovers of tissue, maybe. But their stand marks them as haters of real human beings.

"Scientifically based late-term abortion restrictions would . . . simply protect lives whose humanity is now known."

Third Trimester Abortions Should Be Viewed as Immoral

Gregg Easterbrook

Gregg Easterbrook is a senior editor of the *New Republic*, a contributing editor of the *Atlantic Monthly*, a contributing editor of the *Washington Monthly*, and a visiting fellow at the Brookings Institution. In the following viewpoint he maintains that new scientific evidence strongly supports the view that human personhood begins in the third trimester of pregnancy. In the third trimester, he writes, the fetus begins to exhibit complex brain-wave activity that is similar to that of newborn infants, suggesting that the fetus may be developing consciousness. Easterbrook believes that the onset of brain activity should be used to define when personhood begins. Using this definition, he concludes that early-term abortions should remain legal but that late-term abortions should be strictly regulated.

As you read, consider the following questions:

1. What type of device is used to measure brain activity, according to the author?
2. During which week of pregnancy does the fetus's cerebral cortex become "wired," according to Easterbrook?
3. How do most western European countries view late-term abortion, in the author's words?

No other issue in American politics stands at such an impasse. Decades after *Roe v. Wade* [legalized abortion], the abortion debate remains a clash of absolutes: one side insists that all abortions be permitted, the other that all be prohibited. The stalemate has many and familiar causes, but a critical and little-noticed one is this: Public understanding has not kept pace with scientific discovery. When *Roe* was decided in 1973, medical knowledge of the physiology and neurology of the fetus was surprisingly scant. Law and religion defined our understanding, because science had little to say. That is now changing, and it is time for the abortion debate to change in response. . . .

Complex Brain Activity in the Third Trimester

Over the past decade, pediatric surgeons have learned to conduct within-womb operations on late-term fetuses with correctable congenital conditions. As they operated within the womb, doctors found that the fetus is aware of touch, responds to sound, shows a hormonal stress reaction, and exhibits other qualities associated with mental awareness. "The idea that the late-term fetus cannot feel or sense has been overturned by the last fifteen years of research," says Dr. Nicholas Fisk, a professor of obstetrics at the Imperial College School of Medicine in London.

Most striking are electroencephalogram (EEG) readings of the brain waves of the third-trimester fetus. Until recently, little was known about fetal brain activity because EEG devices do not work unless electrodes are attached to the scalp, which is never done while the fetus is in the womb. But the past decade has seen a fantastic increase in doctors' ability to save babies born prematurely. That in turn has provided a supply of fetal-aged subjects who are out of the womb and in the neonatal intensive care ward, where their EEG readings can be obtained.

EEGs show that third-trimester babies display complex brain activity similar to that found in full-term newborns. The legal and moral implications of this new evidence are enormous. After all, society increasingly uses cessation of brain activity to define when life ends. Why not use the onset of brain activity to define when life begins?

Here is the developmental sequence of human life as suggested by the latest research. After sperm meets egg, the cells spend about a week differentiating and dividing into a zygote. One to two weeks later the zygote implants in the uterine wall, commencing the pregnancy. It is during this initial period that about half of the "conceived" sperm-egg pairings die naturally. Why this happens is not well-understood: one guess is that genetic copying errors occur during the incipient stages of cellular division.

The zygotes that do implant soon transform into embryos. During its early growth, an embryo is sufficiently undifferentiated that it is impossible to distinguish which tissue will end up as part of the new life and which will be discarded as placenta. By about the sixth week the embryo gives way to the fetus, which has a recognizable human shape. (It was during the embryo-fetus transition, Augustine believed, that the soul is acquired, and this was Catholic doctrine for most of the period from the fifth century until 1869.) Also around the sixth week, faint electrical activity can be detected from the fetal nervous system. Some pro-life commentators say this means that brain activity begins during the sixth week, but, according to Dr. Martha Herbert, a neurologist at Massachusetts General Hospital, there is little research to support that claim. Most neurologists assume that electrical activity in the first trimester represents random neuron firings as nerves connect—basically, tiny spasms.

The Beginning of Consciousness

The fetus's heart begins to beat, and by about the twentieth week the fetus can kick. Kicking is probably a spasm, too, at least initially, because the fetal cerebral cortex, the center of voluntary brain function, is not yet "wired," its neurons still nonfunctional. (Readings from 20- to 22-week-old premature babies who died at birth show only very feeble EEG signals.) From the twenty-second week to the twenty-fourth week, connections start to be established between the cortex and the thalamus, the part of the brain that translates thoughts into nervous-system commands. Fetal consciousness seems physically "impossible" before these connections form, says Fisk, of the Imperial College School of Medicine.

At about the twenty-third week the lungs become able to function, and, as a result, 23 weeks is the earliest date at which premature babies have survived. At 24 weeks the third trimester begins, and at about this time, as the cerebral cortex becomes "wired," fetal EEG readings begin to look more and more like those of a newborn. It may be a logical consequence, either of natural selection or of divine creation, that fetal higher brain activity begins at about the time when life outside the mother becomes possible. After all, without brain function, prematurely born fetuses would lack elementary survival skills, such as the ability to root for nourishment.

At about 26 weeks the cell structure of the fetal brain begins to resemble a newborn's, though many changes remain in store. By the twenty-seventh week, according to Dr. Phillip Pearl, a pediatric neurologist at Children's Hospital in Washington, D.C., the fetal EEG reading shows well-organized activity that partly overlaps with the brain activity of adults, although the patterns are far from mature and will continue to change for many weeks. By the thirty-second week, the fetal brain pattern is close to identical to that of a full-term baby.

Summing up, Paul Grobstein, a professor of neurology at Bryn Mawr University, notes, "I think it can be comfortably said that by the late term the brain of the fetus is responding to inputs and generating its own output. The brain by then is reasonably well-developed. But we still don't know what within the fetal brain corresponds to the kind of awareness and experience that you and I have." The fetus may not know it is a baby or have the language-ordered thoughts of adults. But Grobstein points out that from the moment in the third trimester that the brain starts running, the fetus can experience the self/other perceptions that form the basis of human consciousness—since the womb, to it, represents the outside world.

Prohibiting Third-Trimester Abortions

In 1997, the Royal College of Obstetricians and Gynecologists, Britain's equivalent to a panel of the National Academy of Sciences, found that, because new research shows that the fetus has complex brain activity from the third trimester on, "we recommend that practitioners who undertake termination of pregnancy at 24 weeks or later should consider the requirements for feticide or fetal analgesia and sedation." In this usage, "feticide" means killing the fetus the day before the abortion with an injection of potassium that stops the fetus's heart, so that death comes within the womb. Otherwise, the Royal College suggests that doctors anesthetize the fetus before a third-trimester termination—because the fetus will feel the pain of death and may even, in some sense, be aware that it is being killed.

Abortion Is Generally Prohibited in the Third Trimester

The American College of Obstetricians and Gynecologists has defined abortion as "the expulsion or extraction of all (complete) or any part (incomplete) of the placenta or membranes, with or without an abortus, before the 20th week (before 134 days) of gestation." This definition is based on the scientifically-established fact that a developing human organism cannot survive outside the womb before this date and therefore premature birth is not even an elective option. In reality, before the 24th week the chance of a baby's survival outside the womb is almost nil, but doctors use the 20th week as the cut-off because there have been some rare cases of survival at that early a point, but none before, and the degree of organ development that is necessary for survival even to be feasible occurs between 20 and 24 weeks of gestation.

Most abortions are conducted before the 85th day (within the first trimester). An abortion conducted between the 85th and 134th day of a pregnancy (second trimester) is formally called a "late-term abortion." Recent invention in political circles of the term "partial-birth abortion" refers not to abortion at all, but to the killing of a premature (third trimester) baby who is considered to have a remote chance of survival outside the womb. Such a procedure is almost unheard of and is conducted only under the most unusual of circumstances, such as when a baby is already dead, or cannot be prematurely delivered—due to deformity or injury of the womb or birth canal—but must still be removed to save the mother's life. In almost every other case, after the 20th week, "abortion" is neither safe nor necessary—the baby would simply be delivered.

Richard C. Carrier, "Abortion Is Not Immoral and Should Not Be Illegal," www.infidels.org.

If a woman's life is imperiled, sacrificing a third-trimester fetus may be unavoidable. But the American Medical Association (AMA) says late-term abortions to save the mother's life are required only under "extraordinary circumstances"; almost all late-term abortions are elective. In turn, the best estimates suggest that about 750 late-term abortions occur annually in the United States, less than one percent of total abortions. (An estimated 89 percent of U.S. abortions occur in the first trimester, ethically the least perilous time.) Pro-choice advocates sometimes claim that, because less than one percent of abortions are late-term, the issue doesn't matter. But moral dilemmas are not attenuated by percentages: no one would claim that 750 avoidable deaths of adults did not matter.

On paper the whole issue would seem moot, because Supreme Court decisions appear to outlaw late-term abortion except when the woman's life is imperiled. But in practice the current legal regime allows almost any abortion at any time. . . .

It is time to admit what everyone knows and what the new science makes clear: that third-trimester abortion should be very tightly restricted. The hopelessly confusing viability standard should be dropped in favor of a bright line drawn at the start of the third trimester, when complex fetal brain activity begins. Restricting abortion after that point would not undermine the rights granted by *Roe*, because there is no complex brain activity before the third trimester and thus no slippery slope to start down. Scientifically based late-term abortion restrictions would not enter into law poignant but unprovable spiritual assumptions about the spark of life but would simply protect lives whose humanity is now known.

To be sure, restrictions on late-term abortion would harm the rights of American women, but the harm would be small, while the moral foundation of abortion choice overall would be strengthened by removing the taint of late-term abortion. By contrast, restrictions on early abortions would cause tremendous damage to women's freedom while offering only a hazy benefit to the next generation, since so many pregnancies end naturally anyway. There are costs to either trade-off, but they are costs that a decent society can bear.

Follow Europe's Example

Western Europe is instructive in this regard. In most European Union nations, early abortion is not only legal but far less politically contentious than it is here. Yet, in those same countries, late-term abortion is considered infanticide. All European Union nations except France and the United Kingdom ban abortion in the third trimester, except to save the mother's life. And, even where allowed, late-term abortion occurs at one-third the U.S. rate. Western European countries have avoided casting abortion as a duel between irresolvable absolutes. They treat abortion in the first two trimesters as a morally ambiguous private matter, while viewing it in the third trimester as public and morally odious. We should follow their lead. All it requires is knowledge of the new fetal science and a return to the true logic of *Roe*.

"The question . . . is not, 'When does life begin?' but, 'Can it ever be moral for a woman to be pregnant against her will?'"

The Morality of Abortion Does Not Depend on the Stages of Pregnancy

Karen Houppert

Karen Houppert is a freelance journalist who frequently writes on feminist issues. In the following viewpoint she rejects the idea that if an unborn fetus is deemed to be a "person" then abortion is wrong. Specifically, she takes issue with the notion that because third-trimester fetuses exhibit complex brain activity, they are therefore persons. In Houppert's view, the key issue in the abortion debate is not when life begins or when the fetus becomes nearly fully developed but rather whether a woman should be able to control her own body. It is wrong for society to bestow on the fetus any kind of right to life, she argues, because doing so means that women can then be forced to be pregnant against their will.

As you read, consider the following questions:

1. When does Gregg Easterbrook believe a "bright line" should be drawn, as quoted by Houppert?
2. When do women tend to bestow "personhood" on the fetus, according to the author?
3. How does Houppert phrase what she believes is the central question of the abortion controversy?

Karen Houppert, "The Meaning of Life," *The Nation*, vol. 270, March 13, 2000, p. 7. Copyright © 2000 by The Nation Magazine/The Nation Company, Inc. Reproduced by permission.

In January [2000] the Supreme Court announced that it would consider the constitutionality of Nebraska's "partial birth" abortion ban. The Court is stepping into the abortion fray for the first time in eight years to settle a judicial dispute: While the Court of Appeals for the Eighth Circuit has ruled that Nebraska's law is unconstitutional, the Court of Appeals for the Seventh Circuit has ruled that two similar laws in Illinois and Wisconsin are fine.[1]

Legally speaking, "partial birth" abortion laws have been a mess. Since 1995 thirty state legislatures have passed such laws, which deliberately define the term "partial birth" vaguely. Of those laws, twenty-two have become tangled in the courts and have been either completely blocked or severely limited. Although only an estimated 650 women in the United States have this emergency late-term procedure each year (less than 1 percent of all abortions), "partial birth" abortion has taken center stage in the courts, the legislatures and even the presidential race. Those third-trimester abortions that do occur, meanwhile, are almost always a result of fetal anomalies discovered late in a pregnancy or limited access to abortion services—among teens too scared to get parental permission or judicial waivers early enough and women who live in any of the 86 percent of US counties with no abortion facilities.

Trying to Define When Personhood Begins

So it came as news to a lot of people when, in the January 31 [2000] *New Republic*, senior editor Gregg Easterbrook announced that he'd found an easy way to stop the nation's endless nattering on the subject. Easterbrook's silver bullet? Almighty science. "New fetal science may provide a rational, nonideological foundation on which to ground the abortion compromise that currently proves so elusive," he wrote in an article called "What Neither Side Wants You to Know: Abortion and Brain Waves."

Easterbrook's argument goes like this: Abortion should be allowed in the first two trimesters because "new science" shows us that tons of fertilized eggs die off then anyway.

1. The Supreme Court struck down the Nebraska law in June 2000.

"Only about half of all zygotes implant in the uterine wall and become embryos; the others fail to continue dividing and expire," he says. "Of those embryos that do trigger pregnancy, only around 65 percent lead to live births, even with the best prenatal care." Therefore, he says, "it is hard to see why a woman should not be allowed to produce the same effect using artificial means."

Flawed though this reasoning is—hmm, lots of people die of natural causes so shouldn't society be allowed to "produce the same effect using artificial means"?—it is part two of Easterbrook's argument that is most troubling. Forget Catholic doctrine, which says the fetus acquires a soul during week six, he says. Forget common law, which places it at "quickening"; forget religious conservatives, who say life begins at conception; and forget the Supreme Court's standard of fetus "viability." Tiresome arguments all! According to Easterbrook's new science, at twenty-four weeks the fetus's "cerebral cortex becomes 'wired,'" and "fetal EEG readings begin to look more and more like those of a newborn." Easterbrook contends that the "hopelessly confusing viability standard should be dropped in favor of a bright line drawn at the start of the third trimester, when complex fetal brain activity begins."

Simple.

It is at this point that feminists who've been around the block once or twice must fight the temptation to take this earnest neoliberal by the hand and lead him gently back to the point of contention: What does it mean that this fetus acquires "personhood" inside the body of another?

A Woman's Right to Control Her Own Body Is More Important

Memo to Gregg: Yours is that same tiresome argument about when life begins. Randall Terry [founder of Operation Rescue, an anti-abortion group] and his minions call them the "preborn." You've simply modernized, adding the intellectual's imprimatur by invoking science to define "signs of formed humanity."

But get this. Most of us feminists don't even disagree with you. We might quibble with the notion that "personhood" is

A Woman's Right to Control Her Body

Opponents of abortion commonly spend most of their time establishing that the fetus is a person, and hardly any time explaining the step from there to the impermissibility of abortion. Perhaps they think the step too simple and obvious to require much comment. . . . Whatever the explanation, I suggest that the step they take is neither easy nor obvious, that it calls for closer examination than it is commonly given, and that when we do give it this closer examination we shall feel inclined to reject it.

I propose, then, that we grant that the fetus is a person from the moment of conception. How does the argument go from here? Something like this, I take it. Every person has a right to life. So the fetus has a right to life. No doubt the mother has a right to decide what shall happen in and to her body; everyone would grant that. But surely a person's right to life is stronger and more stringent than the mother's right to decide what happens in and to her body, and so outweighs it. So the fetus may not be killed; an abortion may not be performed.

It sounds plausible. But now let me ask you to imagine this. You wake up in the morning and find yourself back to back in bed with an unconscious violinist. A famous unconscious violinist. He has been found to have a fatal kidney ailment, and the Society of Music Lovers has canvassed all the available medical records and found that you alone have the right blood type to help. They have therefore kidnapped you, and last night the violinist's circulatory system was plugged into yours, so that your kidneys can be used to extract poisons from his blood as well as your own. The director of the hospital now tells you, "Look, we're sorry the Society of Music Lovers did this to you—we would never have permitted it if we had known. But still, they did it, and the violinist now is plugged into you. To unplug you would be to kill him. But never mind, it's only for nine months. By then he will have recovered from his ailment, and can safely be unplugged from you." Is it morally incumbent on you to accede to this situation? . . . I imagine you would regard this as outrageous, which suggests that something really is wrong with that plausible-sounding argument I mentioned a moment ago.

Judith Jarvis Thomson, "A Defense of Abortion," *Philosophy and Public Affairs*, Fall 1971.

bestowed at precisely twenty-four weeks when brain waves are first detected on an EEG, because in general, when a pregnancy is a welcome one, we women tend to bestow "personhood" immediately. (We change the way we eat; "You're eating for two now." We pass around sonograms and coo at those ten little "signs of formed humanity." We mourn when we miscarry.)

Though Easterbrook presents his "solution" as new, it's already possible to ban third-trimester abortions under *Roe v. Wade*. And he's just the latest in a long line of liberals obsessed with pinpointing the onset of life. In fact, in a well-known 1985 essay in the *Village Voice* ("Putting Women Back in the Abortion Debate"), Ellen Willis opened by remarking on a new trend. "Once people took for granted that abortion was an issue of sexual politics and morality. Now, abortion is most often discussed as a question of 'life' in the abstract." Typically, arguments about "life" come from the right, but with some regularity they also come from progressives, socialists and liberals, who talk about protecting fetal rights as if they could be separated from women's rights. Each time, the argument is presented as new and provocative. Each time, the messenger is heralded as original and insightful.

Enter Easterbrook. The year is 2000. "Scientifically based late-term abortion restrictions would not enter into law poignant but unprovable spiritual assumptions about the spark of life," he writes, "but would simply protect lives whose humanity is now known."

This is where our jaded feminist gives a weary nod and says, "Remember, this fetus is being carried inside a woman's body. The question," she'd remind him, "is not, 'When does life begin?' but, 'Can it ever be moral for a woman to be pregnant against her will?'"

Periodical Bibliography

The following articles have been selected to supplement the diverse views presented in this chapter.

America	"Standing for the Unborn," May 26, 2003.
Jennifer Baumgardner	"We're Not Sorry, Charlie," *Nation*, February 2, 2004.
Lisa Sowle Cahill	"Realigning Catholic Priorities: Bioethics and the Common Good," *America*, September 13, 2004.
Elden Francis Curtiss	"What Does Donum Vitae Teach Pro-Life Americans?" *Celebrate Life*, January/February 2002.
Clark D. Forsythe	"An Unnecessary Evil," *First Things*, February 2003.
Joan Greenwood	"The New Ethics of Abortion," *Journal of Medical Ethics*, October 2001.
Nat Hentoff	"A Pro-Life Atheist Civil Libertarian," *Free Inquiry*, Fall 2001.
Frances Kissling	"Is There Life After *Roe*? How to Think About the Fetus," *Conscience*, Winter 2004.
Jodie Morse	"Choice and the Post-*Roe* Generation," *Time*, January 27, 2003.
Lorraine V. Murray	"The Least of These," *America*, January 22, 2001.
Anna Quindlen	"Life Begins at Conversation," *Newsweek*, November 29, 2004.
Christine A. Scheller	"A Laughing Child in Exchange for Sin," *Christianity Today*, February 13, 2004.
Sarah Wildman	"New Choice—Big-Tent Abortion Politics," *New Republic*, May 10, 2004.

Does Abortion Benefit Women?

Chapter Preface

Throughout the 1990s a major abortion controversy was whether the so-called "abortion pill" should be available in the United States. The drug, known as RU-486 in Europe and mifepristone in the United States, induces abortion in women who are up to nine weeks pregnant. This type of abortion is known as medical (as opposed to surgical) abortion.

Mifepristone is different from emergency contraception, or so-called "morning after" pills, although the two are often confused. Emergency contraceptives such as the brand-name pill Plan B prevent a pregnancy if taken soon after sex, while mifepristone is used to terminate pregnancy, usually weeks after it has begun.

Mifepristone became widely available in Europe in 1991 and was hailed by pro-choice groups as a safe and effective early abortion option. However, the U.S. Food and Drug Administration (FDA) banned the drug in 1989, partly because of concerns over its safety and partly because of pressure from anti-abortion groups. After a decade of political debate and several clinical trials, the FDA approved the drug in September 2000, and since then it has been available in the United States.

Arguments about the safety of mifepristone made headlines again in September 2003, when eighteen-year-old Holly Patterson died of an infection one week after taking the drug. Anti-abortion writers such as columnist Brent Bozell called for a renewed ban on mifepristone, charging that "the Clinton administration rushed the approval of RU-486 through the Food and Drug Administration." Defenders of the drug, however, argue that while there is a risk of infection associated with any type of abortion, the risk is small and presents no reason to prohibit the use of mifepristone. "It's been used around the world for more than ten years with several million pregnancy terminations, with a remarkable safety record," claims Dr. Philip Darney of San Francisco General Hospital.

The health and emotional effects of abortion continue to be a topic of dispute in the abortion debate. The authors in the following chapter offer their views on how abortion affects women.

| "*As abortion providers, our interaction with a woman . . . is usually an opportunity to provide an immediate health benefit and reinforce positive health behaviors.*"

Access to Safe and Legal Abortion Benefits Women

Felicia H. Stewart and Philip D. Darney

Felicia H. Stewart is codirector of the Center for Reproductive Health Research and Policy, and Philip D. Darney is chief of obstetrics, gynecology, and reproductive sciences at San Francisco General Hospital. They maintain in the following viewpoint that abortion providers benefit women. Access to safe and legal abortion, they argue, has lowered maternal mortality rates. In addition, they contend that legal abortion has a positive impact on women since it gives them control over whether and when they will become mothers. Access to safe, legal abortion, they conclude, gives women the power to resolve what might be the biggest problem they ever face—unwanted pregnancy.

As you read, consider the following questions:

1. How do antichoice arguments often stereotype women, in the authors' view?
2. What is the abortion rate in the United States for women ages fifteen to forty, as reported by Stewart and Darney?
3. What are some of the religious organizations that the authors list as being in support of safe and legal access to abortion?

Felicia H. Stewart and Philip D. Darney, "Abortion: Teaching Why as Well as How," *Perspectives on Sexual and Reproductive Health*, vol. 35, January/February 2003. Copyright © 2003 by The Alan Guttmacher Institute. Reproduced by permission.

As clinicians, scientists and educators, we are not accustomed to talking about our values and the spiritual aspects of what we do—particularly as regards offering and teaching about abortion care. Many of us feel shy about expressing personal feelings and uncertain about how nonscientific topics like morality and religion can appropriately be raised in a teaching setting. Nevertheless, many of our students would appreciate help with responding to religious criticism; they deserve an honest attempt to explain why we teach and provide abortion services, and why they might want to consider providing these services in their future practices.

For both of us, and for many of our colleagues, providing abortion care has been a positive career decision—not a negative one or one based on duty. It is positive because this service matters so much to the individual women for whom we provide care, and often to their partners and children as well. Providing abortion in our own communities connects our work with an issue of worldwide importance, because confronting at home the efforts to intimidate providers and limit access to abortion is part of an effort to overturn laws, policies and traditions around the world that control and harm women's reproductive lives.

Many medical educators, and even legislators, have come to recognize the importance of teaching about abortion, especially the technical skills involved—the "how." Medical and health science students also need education about the "who," "what," "when," "where" and, especially, "why" aspects of abortion. The exclusion of abortion from the services provided to women in teaching hospitals has meant that many students complete their training with little or no experience providing abortion care. Students may be unaware of the importance of this service in many women's lives. Furthermore, they may be unprepared to participate knowledgeably in the development of women's health programs, in public policy debate on abortion or even in discussions of abortion within their own institutions.

For many technical medical skills, the public health, ethical and historical aspects of care are integrated into the preclinical curriculum. However, in the case of abortion, it is not safe to assume that the curriculum includes these topics. In addition, clinical training schedules typically have so little time and place so much emphasis on building technical competence that ancillary education may not receive much attention. Furthermore, since abortion patients often receive counseling and education from lay staff and not from clinicians, students learning how to perform abortions may not have an opportunity to learn firsthand why individual women seek such services. And because of the religious and social context of abortion, the individual clinician's understanding of "why" is likely to be critical to whether he or she decides to provide abortion services.

Despite a lack of models for teaching "why," we have begun to address this with our students. Unlike their teachers, most students and residents today do not remember abortion practices before *Roe v. Wade* [made abortion legal], or the public debate that led to abortion law reform. They have been busy learning science and medicine, and have had little opportunity to consider these issues. By summarizing our initial attempts to identify key points, we hope to encourage other colleagues to join the task and help shape a new and strong curriculum component for teaching "why."

Beyond Public Health

The public health aspects of abortion provide a clear starting place. A large body of scientific evidence creates a compelling argument for the public health importance of universal access to safe, legal abortion services. Maternal morbidity and mortality rates decline promptly when safe abortion services are made available, and in many parts of the world, unsafe abortion still ranks as a leading cause of death and injury among women. Concern about public health was a major focus of the initial state-by-state efforts in the 1950s and 1960s to reform abortion laws. Physicians led reform campaigns that won broad support from the medical community. Today, the public health perspective is an important reason for the strong and continued support for legal abortion from many medical organizations, including the American College of Obstetricians and Gynecologists, the American Medical Association and the American Public Health Association.

A public health framework alone, however, may not be

helpful to the student who encounters challenging moral or religious questions about abortion. In addition, considering abortion solely as a public health issue has the potential pitfall of reinforcing the view of abortion as a necessary but distasteful task. This has been a common view among clinicians whose involvement with abortion policy issues began during the reform era, and it may have contributed to the professional marginalization of abortion services and providers in the subsequent three decades. A "duty to do your share" approach is unlikely to be an appealing or effective motivation for students deciding whether to provide abortion services in the future.

In moving beyond the public health benefits of abortion, it seems appropriate to focus first on the importance of abortion access to individual women. The decision to become a mother has profound implications for the life and health of the woman. In an essay in the *New York Times*, Dr. Elizabeth Karlin, an abortion provider, eloquently expressed her moral conviction about taking the responsibilities of parenthood very seriously and how abortion plays a part: "I am an abortion practitioner because of my utmost respect for motherhood. . . . I am convinced that being a mother is the hardest job there is. . . . Even more than performing a religious ritual, being a mother requires precise abilities, arrangements, resources, and a community of support. Motherhood, then, is the true sacrament, and helping make it so is the essence of my work."

Taking Motherhood Seriously

Women seeking abortions likewise take motherhood seriously. For some, the impact on family members, especially their children, is a primary consideration. For a few, health problems are the most important factor. And for many others, relationship, financial and educational issues are paramount. In our experience, however, women typically approach the decision with careful thought, and for many women (and couples), the moral importance of being the best parents they can be is a significant issue. They are determined to avoid parenthood in a situation that would make fulfilling their moral obligation unlikely or impossible. Although it may seem obvious, the weight of the decision about parenthood is an important topic for discussion because antichoice arguments often stereotype women who decide to terminate pregnancies as selfish and irresponsible.

Roe v. Wade Has Benefited Women

By invalidating laws that forced women to resort to back-alley abortion, *Roe* saved women's lives. According to one estimate made before 1973, "more than five thousand women may have died [per year] as a direct result [of criminal abortions]. Many deaths from illegal abortion may go unlabeled as such because of careless or casual autopsies and the lack of experience and ability of autopsy surgeons." Since the legalization of abortion in 1973, the safety of abortion has increased dramatically. The number of deaths per 100,000 legal abortion procedures declined from 4.1 to 0.6 between 1973 and 1997. In addition, *Roe* has improved the quality of many women's lives. Although most women welcome pregnancy, childbirth and the responsibilities of raising a child at some period in their lives, few events can more dramatically constrain a woman's opportunities than an unplanned child. Because childbirth and pregnancy substantially affect a woman's educational prospects, employment opportunities, and self-determination, restrictive abortion laws narrowly circumscribed women's role in society and hindered women from defining their paths through life in the most basic of ways. In the 31 years since *Roe*, the variety and level of women's achievements have reached unprecedented heights. The Supreme Court observed that the ability of women to participate equally in the economic and social life of the nation has been facilitated by their ability to control their reproductive lives.

NARAL Pro-Choice America, "*Roe v. Wade* and the Right to Choose," www.prochoiceamerica.org, January 1, 2004.

It is true that some women seeking abortions do not seem to be making a careful decision or are unable to do so. However, consider these statistics: The U.S. annual abortion rate of 21 per 1,000 women aged 15–40 means that about 60 abortions occur for every 100 women over the roughly 35 years of their reproductive lives. With so many women deciding to have an abortion, it is hard to imagine that a single stereotype includes them all. Women who have abortions are our neighbors, friends, mothers, sisters and daughters.

Although the U.S. abortion rate is lower than the world-wide average rate of 35 per 1,000 women, it is higher than rates in most other developed countries. Does this difference indicate that American women are somehow less responsible or moral? Would restricted access to abortion lower the abortion rate? There is no evidence to support these conclusions. Practical steps to reduce unintended pregnancies and, therefore, the need for abortions are easy to identify: Women and men in the United States are much less likely to have had comprehensive sexuality education and more likely to face economic obstacles in seeking contraceptive care than their counterparts in developed countries with lower abortion rates. Furthermore, public funding in the United States covers family planning services for fewer than half of the low-income couples who need them.

Health Benefits of Abortion

As abortion providers, our interaction with a woman may be brief, but it is usually an opportunity to provide an immediate health benefit and reinforce positive health behaviors. Women planning their contraceptive use after an abortion often need to solve problems they have had with side effects or method use so as to improve their success with pregnancy prevention. For many young women, seeking an abortion is the first important health decision they have had to make; recognition of their own abilities to take charge of their health can serve as a basis for other important health decisions, such as practicing contraception.

It may be surprising to see "immediate health benefit" listed as one of the positive aspects of abortion care. Most women deciding what to do about an unintended pregnancy do not consider the relative health risks for full-term pregnancy versus early abortion, but clinicians recognize very significant differences. Women who continue their pregnancy to term have at least 10 times the risk of death of those who choose abortion, as well as a significantly higher risk of morbidity—including a 20% risk for abdominal surgery (i.e., cesarean delivery). Is there any other medical situation in which a clinician would recommend that an option involving so much greater risk always be preferred?

But the decision to end a pregnancy is not directly parallel to other medical decisions: If a woman does not choose abortion, she will likely deliver a healthy baby, so the decision involves a potential life. Yet, religious opposition to abortion often considers only the potential life and ignores the woman's life and health risks. Women surely deserve some consideration in religious as well as medical thinking.

Just how the significance of potential life should be weighed in relation to the woman's (and existing family's) health and life provokes considerable disagreement. Many religious groups have concluded that choosing abortion can be a moral decision consonant with religious teachings, and oppose efforts to impose legal or governmental interference. Examples include the American Baptist Churches, U.S.A.; Episcopal Church; Lutheran Church in America; Presbyterian Church, U.S.A.; Reorganized Church of Jesus Christ of Latter-Day Saints; Union of American Hebrew Congregations; Unitarian Universalist Association; United Church of Christ; and United Methodist Church.

However, several religious bodies, such as the Roman Catholic Church and certain fundamentalist Christian groups, hold that abortion for any reason is unacceptable, or that it can be justified only in very limited situations. Although this conclusion represents the beliefs of a small minority of the U.S. public, the leaders of these religions have been extensively involved in efforts to restrict access to abortion services as a matter of public policy. They have been instrumental in achieving the virtual elimination of public funding for abortion services in many states, as well as for women who are federal employees or in the U.S. military. Many of these religious leaders also oppose the practice of contraception and comprehensive sexuality education for youth, and share the belief that pregnancy and childbearing should be determined by divine control. Included in this group are the leadership of the Catholic Church, Church of Jesus Christ of Latter-Day Saints, Lutheran Church–Missouri Synod and Southern Baptist Church.

Abortion Since *Roe*

The legal status of abortion is a related question. The 1973 decisions by the Supreme Court in *Roe v. Wade* and *Doe v.*

Bolton made abortion legal throughout the country, and eliminated state requirements for justifying abortion on medical or psychiatric grounds. The Court ruled in *Roe* that during the first trimester, "the abortion decision and its effectuation must be left to the medical judgment of the pregnant woman's attending physician," and that during the second trimester, "the state, in promoting its interest in the health of the mother, may . . . regulate the abortion procedure in ways that are reasonably related to maternal health." During the last trimester—after about 24 weeks—the Court ruled that "a state, in promoting its interest in the potentiality of human life, may . . . regulate, and even proscribe, abortion except where it is necessary, in appropriate medical judgment, for the preservation of the life or health of the mother."

In 1992, the Supreme Court discarded the trimester framework in favor of a more lenient standard for determining the constitutionality of abortion restrictions: whether they impose an "undue burden" on the woman. At the same time, the Court reaffirmed "the essential holding of *Roe v. Wade* that prior to fetal viability, a woman has a constitutional right to obtain an abortion." Since *Roe*, the Court has upheld a variety of state restrictions on access to abortion, such as waiting periods and mandatory parental involvement for minors, and a ban on the use of federal funds for abortions for poor women under most circumstances. However, unless *Roe* is overturned, abortion will remain legal throughout the United States.

As much as safe abortion care means to American women, it means even more to women in less-affluent countries. Current U.S. policies for international aid include a gag rule intended to stifle efforts in other countries to establish access to safe, legal abortion; at the same time, family planning aid has been curtailed. This means that basic prevention services and contraceptives are not widely available in many countries, and unintended pregnancy rates, which are already high, remain so. In less-affluent countries, maternal death is a substantial health risk, and the most powerful steps to reduce it include ensuring access to contraceptives and safe abortion care. Our restrictive policies and practices have found their way to countries where the women affected are among the poorest and least powerful in the world; the health consequences are severe, and often life-threatening. Working here to change restrictive policies and laws, and to address the toxic political dialogue, could help poor women in the United States and women in developing countries as well. It seems the least we can do.

Unfortunately, even in the United States, many women seeking abortion care do not expect to find supportive or humane care. When they do find kindness, they are truly appreciative. An abortion provider interviewed in the mid-1990s expressed a common sentiment: "There is nothing else I do in my medical practice where people look me in the eye, in quite the same way, and say 'thank you.' I feel I am empowering women."

A Clear Benefit

For both of us, abortion has been a priority throughout our careers. It has been and is a positive and fulfilling professional and personal focus. Normally, a simple medical task does not matter so much, but this one does. The experience of women seeking abortion is so burdened by intimidation and shame that it takes a serious dose of kindness, respect and support to overcome the harmful effects of the political and social context in which we all live. Abortion care is one of the few medical services we provide that can quickly and effectively resolve a major problem in an individual woman's life. We can make sure that the experience that women or couples have validates them as human beings, supports their willingness to take charge of their lives and recognizes that decisions about pregnancy and parenthood are important moral choices.

> *"Initially hailed as a woman's ticket out of the kitchen and into the boardroom, abortion today has become increasingly associated with sexual irresponsibility and moral degradation."*

Legalized Abortion Has Harmed Women

Candace C. Crandall

Candace C. Crandall is an adjunct fellow with the National Center for Public Policy Research in Washington, D.C. In the following viewpoint she argues that legalized abortion has failed to benefit women and society. Whereas abortion was supposed to curb illegitimate births among the poor, Crandall points out that rates of illegitimacy are much higher now than they were in the 1970s. She also argues that abortion is no safer today than it was prior to *Roe v. Wade* because most competent physicians refuse to perform abortions. Instead of viewing abortion as something that empowers women, Crandall concludes, society now looks on abortion with scorn and distaste.

As you read, consider the following questions:

1. What percent of births were to umarried mothers in 1970 as compared to 2003, according to Crandall?
2. How many abortion-related deaths were there in 1972, according to the author?
3. In the 1998 Wirthlin poll that Crandall cites, what percentage of women said that legal abortion is not necessary for them to pursue their career goals?

In the long and arduous fight leading up to *Roe v. Wade* [which made abortion legal], the one thing feminists were most passionate about was their belief that unrestricted access to abortion was indispensable to achieving gender equality. Betty Friedan in 1972 promised that legalizing abortion would make women whole. Advocacy groups, including the National Organization for Women, the National Association for the Repeal of Abortion Laws (now the National Abortion and Reproductive Rights Action League), and the President's Advisory Council on the Status of Women, stood adamantly opposed to any limits, claiming regulation would violate a woman's right to control her body.

When one looks at the data today, noting that half of all women undergoing abortion in 2002 will be having at least their second, and that one of every five will be having at least her third, a number of highly descriptive thoughts come to mind. "In control" isn't one of them.

The successful push for unrestricted abortion on demand, nationwide, rested on two factors. The first was fortuitous timing. In the 1960s, the nation was caught up in the turmoil of three great social movements: civil rights, with its emphasis on effecting sweeping political change via the courts; feminism, with its promise to empower the victims of very real social and economic injustice; and environmentalism, which had fostered nationwide hysteria with claims of an imminent population disaster. The point at which the tenets of these three movements converged was abortion.

Empty Promises

The second and more important factor was packaging. Abortion, from the onset, was not a health issue; it was politics. And politics is personal. In 1968, public opinion polls revealed scant support for legalizing abortion. Few Americans anticipated any personal benefit and many had serious moral concerns. But over the next five years, abortion rights advocates overcame Americans' qualms with repeated assurances that when every child was a "wanted" child, broad social benefits would ensue.

According to this argument, illegitimacy would become a thing of the past. Women who found themselves inconveniently pregnant could obtain an abortion and remain in school or in the workforce. Couples would no longer be trapped into miserable, forced marriages. Children would no longer be battered by parents resentful that they were "unplanned."

With an implied reduction in welfare and social services, abortion was transformed in the early 1970s from a moral question into a pocketbook issue. Senator Jacob Javits, for example, described New York's decision to legalize abortion as "a significant step forward in dealing with the human problems of our state."

Members of the Commission on Population Growth, established by President Richard Nixon in 1970, thought so too. In the second of three reports, issued in March 1972, they called for Medicaid-funded abortions as necessary weapons in the war on poverty, noting that "unwanted fertility is highest among those whose levels of education and income are lowest."

This line of thinking already had powerful support from *The Population Bomb*, the 1968 bestselling book by Stanford biologist Paul Ehrlich. Ehrlich, who cofounded the group Zero Population Growth, warned that humans were rapidly populating themselves out of existence. Within slightly more than a decade, he wrote, all ocean life would die of DDT poisoning. Thousands would perish in smog disasters in New York and Los Angeles. Life expectancy in the United States would plunge to just forty-two years, as pollution-induced cancer epidemics decimated the population.

To much of the public, these forecasts seemed frighteningly plausible. Press reports told of earnest young college girls having themselves surgically sterilized rather than risk bringing any more children into an already overcrowded world. In a controversial two-part episode of the popular CBS sitcom *Maude*, broadcast in 1972, the title character chooses to have an abortion. A *New York Times* reporter later revealed that the show had been prompted by a $5,000 prize offered by the Population Institute for the best prime-time script concerning population control.

Abortion rights advocates, employing the rhetoric of equality, were quick to point out that wealthy women could always obtain a safe abortion, legal or not. Extending access to poor women simply corrected a social injustice. The larger reality, given the environmental scare, was a bit different. If all humanity was sitting on an increasingly overcrowded life raft, many Americans reasoned that it might be unwise to let "the poor" occupy too big a corner. By 1972, Americans were increasingly drawn to the banner of "choice."

But did the nation benefit? Are American women more free?

Women Are Not Better Off

Paul Ehrlich, a genuine expert on the Checkerspot butterfly, was not such an expert on human populations, as it turned out. His forecasts of impending disaster from overpopulation were never remotely realistic. But neither was the assumption that America could abort poverty out of existence.

Illegitimacy, far from disappearing, has become a serious social problem. In 1970, just 10.7 percent of all births were to unmarried mothers. By 1975, after *Roe*, the illegitimacy rate in the United States had jumped to 14.5 percent. Nearly 70 percent of black children and 33 percent of all children are born out of wedlock today [2003]. Divorce rates have multiplied, as have reported incidences of child abuse.

What about the familiar refrain that abortion should be a matter between a woman and "her" doctor, the so-called right to privacy? *Roe* hinged on this issue. The reality, today as in 1972, is that a woman's personal physician is unlikely to perform abortions. Two surveys—one by the American College of Obstetrics and Gynecologists in 1985, the other by the Kaiser Family Foundation in 1995—found that two-thirds of the obstetricians and gynecologists in practice in the United States, especially women and those under forty, refuse to do abortions under any circumstances. The reasons offered only rarely had to do with public pressure from anti-abortion activists. Most cited religious scruples or simply said they didn't like doing abortions. Of the one-third that do perform abortions, a majority perform four or fewer per month. That leaves most to specialized abortion clinics that offer women with unplanned pregnancies little in the way of counseling or emotional support.

The Myth of "Back-Alley Butchers"

Of course, the most powerful of the pro-choice arguments was that failure to legalize abortion would leave five to ten thousand women a year bleeding to death from coat-hanger abortions or dying from systemic infections incurred at the hands of "back-alley butchers."

Had anyone bothered to research that claim, then or since, they would have learned that every aspect of it was a myth. Death rates from infections and all types of surgeries, including illegal abortions, had already fallen precipitously after World War II, when antibiotics finally became available to the general public. But at no time, even before penicillin and sulfa drugs, had the number of abortion fatalities come anywhere close to the five thousand to ten thousand figure most often cited.

Support for Legal Abortion Is Declining Among Women

In January 2003, Princeton Survey Research Associates concluded a poll of women on abortion and other women's issues. The following chart shows respondents' answers to the question, "Which one of the following statements comes closest to your own view on abortion?" Results from the 2003 poll are shown together with results from an earlier poll conducted in January 2001.

	2003	2001
Should be generally available	30%	34%
Should be available under stricter limits	17	19
Should only be available in cases of rape, incest, or to save the woman's life	34	31
Should not be permitted at all	17	14
Don't know	2	2

Center for Gender Equality, *Progress and Perils: How Gender Issues Unite and Divide Women, Part Two*, April 7, 2003.

In 1940, the National Center for Health Statistics confirmed just 1,313 deaths from illegal abortions, most of them from infection. As antibiotics became available and surgical techniques improved generally, abortion-related deaths fell sharply: 159 deaths in 1966, forty-one in 1972, the year before *Roe*.

Activists contend that most deaths were covered up. But if so, one would still have expected to see a decline in the overall death rate among women after 1973, when abortion became legal nationwide. According to Centers for Disease Control statistics, the death rate among women aged fifteen to thirty-four, the group that today accounts for 94 percent of all abortions in the United States, saw no significant change in the years immediately after *Roe*.

Nor were the abortionists of the 1950s and '60s necessarily untrained: Dr. Mary Calderone, a former medical director for Planned Parenthood, estimated in the *American Journal of Public Health* in 1960 that nine out of ten illegal abortions were already being performed by licensed doctors.

In this there is no little irony. Prior to *Roe v. Wade*, the fact that these doctors were breaking the law kept the numbers of abortions relatively low—as few as 200,000 a year by some estimates—and effectively discouraged most from taking unnecessary risks. Legalization removed that constraint. An unscrupulous abortion doctor could now advertise openly, confident that he would be shielded by abortion rights rhetoric that uniformly proclaimed him a hero, even if his motives were something other than compassion.

Only a year after abortion was legalized in New York state in 1970, writer Susan Edmiston noted with alarm in the *New York Times Magazine* that state health department officials were failing to supervise the numerous abortion clinics that had sprung up throughout the city, establish accurate data collection, or take any action on complaints that were already flooding in. Reporters were turning up similar problems in Los Angeles and the District of Columbia.

Stories like these have been consistently ignored. In 1974, the *Detroit Free Press* found unsafe, unlicensed abortion clinics proliferating in the Detroit area. In 1978, a five-month investigation by the *Chicago Sun-Times* uncovered dangerous medical practices at abortion clinics along Chicago's Michigan Avenue. In 1991, after several gruesome New York abortion cases made national headlines, the *New York Times*, in a front page article, found "filth" and "butchery" at dozens of shabby, unlicensed clinics tucked away behind storefronts or—to evade state regulators—operating out of ordinary-looking doctors' offices, most often in poor neighborhoods.

How much bad medicine is glossed over in the name of choice isn't known. It's impolitic for health agencies to keep good data on deaths and injuries at abortion clinics. And since the much publicized shootings at these clinics, newspapers have shown a reluctance even to report such events. But anyone can sit down at a computer, as I did, and pull up hundreds of newspaper accounts documenting a long history of death, injury, and fraud at walk-in abortion clinics in Atlanta, Houston, St. Louis, Miami, Boston, Los Angeles, Chicago, Detroit, Birmingham, Kansas City, and many other cities. In this atmosphere, supporters' repeated references to abortion as a "vital health service" and to attempts to regulate clinics as "threats to women's safety" begin to ring hollow.

The Turning Tide of Public Opinion

The past decade has been an especially tough one for the abortion rights movement; morale has visibly collapsed. Six years ago, a hard-fought and very public congressional debate over so-called partial-birth abortions—a procedure in which the physician partly delivers a late-term fetus feet first, then kills it by piercing its skull with scissors, attaching a high-powered suction device and sucking out its brain—revealed not only a disturbing brutality toward the unborn but also the widespread occurrence in this country of second- and third-trimester abortions. Facing a horrified public, abortion rights advocates remained rigid ideologues.

With abortion becoming increasingly controversial and the vast majority of doctors reluctant to participate—or medical schools even to teach abortion techniques—advocates turned to RU-486 and other abortion-inducing drugs. Now claims of a too quick approval of RU-486 by the Food and Drug Administration and reports of deaths among seemingly healthy women who used the drug are raising alarms. And this type of abortion, in which the dead fetus is passed in the toilet or shower, with the woman herself as sole witness, may be even more emotionally traumatic than the various surgical procedures. Chemically induced abortions certainly do nothing to reassure the public that abortion is "humane."

Some of abortion's most ardent supporters are expressing doubts. *Roe* poster girl Norma McCorvey, overwhelmed by feelings of guilt, defected in 1996. Germaine Greer, though still holding tight to feminist ideology, complained in her 1999 book *The Whole Woman* that abortion had become just one more oppression—this time from a male-dominated medical establishment that failed to inform women of the risks. She should know. By her own admission, several abortions have left her sterile.

For advocates of choice, surveys of public opinion have become more and more grim. A 1998 Wirthlin poll found that 58 percent of American women felt that abortion had hindered their relationships with men, and 70 percent of men and women believed that legal abortion is not necessary for women to pursue various educational and career goals. A January 1999 survey of 275,811 incoming college freshmen by the Higher Education Research Institute showed that just 52.5 percent of men and 49.5 percent of women thought abortion should be legal—a decline of 14 percentage points since 1990 in an age group typically more pro-choice than any other. In 2000, a *Los Angeles Times* poll showed that just 43 percent of Americans support a continuation of *Roe v. Wade*, down from 56 percent in 1991.

In the last presidential race, while 27 percent of those polled by the *Los Angeles Times* said they were more likely to vote for George W. Bush because he was pro-life, just 18 percent said the same for Al Gore because he was pro-choice.

Nationwide, the number of abortions has been dropping since 1990. But a potentially more significant number was announced this past summer [2002] by the U.S. Census Bureau. Drawing on year 2000 data, the Bureau reported that for the first time in three decades the U.S. birth rate is up. Kids are no longer being regarded as a threat to the planet or Mom's ball and chain. Where the two-child limit was once the hallmark of social responsibility, young couples are opting for more.

Initially hailed as a woman's ticket out of the kitchen and into the boardroom, abortion today has become increasingly associated with sexual irresponsibility and moral degradation. From a proclamation of independence, a woman's admission that she has had an abortion has now become the kind of public announcement that makes men, and other women, cringe, regardless of their politics.

The ability of abortion to galvanize public opinion, to claim influence over election outcomes, is over. Americans looked at *Roe v. Wade* and found nothing in it for them. Should the opportunity arise, the nation may finally be ready to see the abortion issue returned to the state legislatures, where it should have remained some thirty years ago.

"In North America . . . there is a pronounced bias against reporting bad news about induced abortion."

Abortion Harms Women's Health

Ian Gentles

Ian Gentles is a professor of history at York University's Glendon College in Toronto and the coauthor of *Women's Health After Abortion: The Medical and Psychological Evidence*, which argues that the health risks of abortion are downplayed in the United States. In the following viewpoint Gentles summarizes some of the main arguments of his book. According to him, abortion is associated with an increased risk of breast and other cancers, sterility, pelvic inflammatory disease, and complications with future pregnancies. Gentles believes that reporting on the health risks of abortion has become taboo in the United States because special interests do not want abortion banned.

As you read, consider the following questions:

1. How much greater was the risk of breast cancer among women who had abortions compared with those who did not, according to the study by the National Cancer Institute that Gentles cites?
2. How much more likely are women to have a premature birth if they have previously had an abortion, according to the author?
3. What is the goal of most of the researchers who conduct post-abortion research, in Gentles's opinion?

[In 2002] a great deal of anxiety was provoked in the media by the publication of a medical report on the long-term consequences of hormone replacement therapy for women. Among the several negative effects of HRT, the one that caused the greatest distress was the increased risk—about 25 per cent—of breast cancer. The incidence of breast cancer among women has certainly risen alarmingly in the past three decades. Many explanations for this rise have been suggested: a more polluted environment, changes in diet, smoking, the postponement of childbearing, the contraceptive pill, and other drug therapies.

The Link Between Abortion and Breast Cancer

But the media have paid almost no attention to the many studies that have documented a significantly higher incidence of breast cancer among women who have abortions, in particular those who abort their first pregnancy before the age of 20. At least 27 studies in ten countries have discovered an increased risk of 30 per cent—significantly higher than the increased risk of 25 per cent reported in the single study of the effects of HRT.

Strange to say, the authors and sponsors of several of these studies have shied away from the implications of their findings. The National Cancer Institute in the U.S., for example, sponsored a major study which showed a 36 per cent increased risk (rising to a disturbing 50 per cent among women under 20 who abort their first pregnancy) of breast cancer among women who undergo abortions. In fact, given that young women who carry their first pregnancy to term *reduce* their chances of breast cancer by 30 per cent, the consequences are even more dramatic. The lifetime chances of a woman in North America being diagnosed with breast cancer are currently about ten per cent. A woman who has a child before age 20 has a seven per cent chance. On the other hand, if she aborts that first early pregnancy, she more than doubles her lifetime chances to fifteen per cent. Yet the National Cancer Institute, and other establishment voices such as the prestigious *New England Journal of Medicine* stoutly continue to deny that there is any link between abortion and breast cancer.

Curiously, the establishment on the other side of the ocean is much less reluctant to recognize the link. In April 2000, Britain's Royal College of Obstetricians and Gynecologists acknowledged that studies demonstrating the abortion-breast cancer link "could not be disregarded." Writing in the London *Times* a year later, Dr. Thomas Stuttaford declared that "an unusually high proportion" of the women diagnosed with breast cancer in the U.K. each year "had an abortion before eventually starting a family. Such women are up to four times more likely to develop breast cancer."

There are solid physiological reasons for the association between induced abortion and the later development of breast cancer which have to do with the hormonal effects of pregnancy on a woman's breast tissue. A surge of the hormone oestradiol at conception reaches twentyfold in the first trimester, triggering an explosive growth of breast tissue—a period when breast cells are most likely to be affected by carcinogens. When a woman completes her first full pregnancy, further hormonal changes propel these newly produced breast cells through a state of differentiation, a natural maturing process that greatly reduces the risk of future breast cancer. An early, abrupt termination of pregnancy by abortion arrests this process before the cancer-reducing evolution of hormone release can occur, leaving a large population of dangerously-stimulated breast tissue cells in place, enormously raising future cancer risk. On the other hand, ". . . an early first, full-term pregnancy would provide the greatest protection against breast cancer by drastically reducing, early on, the presence of undifferentiated and hence vulnerable breast cells, thereby decreasing the risk of subsequent transformation." A fascinating animal study supports this line of reasoning. Two groups of rats were exposed to a chemical carcinogen before mating. The group that carried a first pregnancy to term developed mammary tumours at a rate of six per cent. The group whose pregnancies were aborted, however, developed mammary tumours at an astounding rate of 78 per cent.

These are among several dramatic findings dredged up from the obscurity of scientific journals and presented in *Women's Health After Abortion: The Medical and Psychological*

Evidence, a new book I co-authored with Elizabeth Ring-Cassidy. In it, we review and summarize over 500 studies which have appeared in medical and professional journals, most of them over the past twenty years. What follows here is a brief overview of our work.

Other Cancers and Maternal Mortality

Cancers of the cervix, ovaries and rectums. Research in this area is in its early stages, but a few studies from the past decade point to a link between abortion and subsequent cancers of the reproductive system, as well as colorectal cancer. Cervical cancer in particular seems to be directly associated with induced abortion. Studies of cancer of the ovary have presented conflicting evidence. A strong association has been discovered between abortion and cancer of the rectum. What is remarkable is that with the increase in cancers of the breast and reproductive system in women over the past thirty years, there has as yet been so little interest in investigating the link with induced abortion. Despite the overwhelming weight of the studies pointing to such a link, their conclusions have been generally ignored by the research establishments in North America. The rationale for this may be that for some it is more important for abortion to remain accessible than for women to be informed about a clear threat to their health. Thus, the politicized and controversial nature of the subject, and the desire of some powerful groups to keep abortion "safe, simple, and easily available," have militated against the objective consideration of data pointing strongly to a link between abortion and various cancers.

Maternal mortality. In both Canada and the U.S. there is a general and systematic underreporting of maternal deaths, whether from abortion, pregnancy, or during delivery. Not least among the reasons for this is the fact that more and more abortions are now performed in free-standing clinics. A woman whose post-abortion condition is life threatening generally goes to a hospital, not back to the clinic. The attending emergency room doctor may not record a subsequent death as resulting from an abortion. The practice of coding the immediate rather than the underlying cause of death also causes underreporting: an induced abortion may result in bleeding, embolism, cardiac arrest or infection, or it may lead to a subsequent ectopic pregnancy. But the death certificate of a woman who dies from these conditions may make no reference to abortion.

A recent, large-scale Scandinavian study found that within one year of the end of a pregnancy, women who had induced abortions suffered a mortality rate that was almost four times greater than that for women who delivered their babies. And their rate of suicide was six times greater. A recent study in Wales found that women who had induced abortions were 2.25 times more likely to commit suicide than women admitted for normal delivery. A large-scale California study just recently published reported similar findings. These studies, using record linkage and involving many hundreds of thousands of cases, authoritatively refute the oft-repeated fiction that induced abortion is safer for women than giving birth.

Lack of Research on Abortion's Health Effects

Approximately 40 percent of American women under 45 have had at least one abortion. Twenty-five percent of all pregnancies end in abortion. Since the legalization of abortion in 1973, over 40 million abortions have taken place. Yet no comprehensive data exists concerning the impact of abortion on women. Consider that the federal government has in place mechanisms to track just about every other medical procedure, but it chooses not to follow this one. . . .

Surely a medical procedure that affects over one million women a year would be worthy of careful monitoring—unless the lives and health of these women are expected to be sacrificed to a particular political ideology.

For every other medical procedure, health-care providers must inform patients about the benefits and risks of the treatment. In the case of abortion, a woman's right to privacy means that she is so isolated in her decision that she is not even given full knowledge of the treatment she has "chosen."

Pia de Solenni, "Hearing Women," www.nationalreview.com, March 9, 2004.

Ectopic pregnancy. While overall health has generally improved in the past century, there has been a disturbing rise in ectopic pregnancies [in which a fertilized egg implants outside the uterus, usually in the fallopian tubes]. Between 1970 and 1990 they doubled, trebled or quadrupled in frequency, depending on the country, so that they now account for two per cent of all pregnancies in the areas studied. The rise of ectopic pregnancy coincides almost exactly with the steep rise in the frequency of induced abortion during the same period. Studies from Italy, Japan, Yugoslavia and the U.S. have documented a much higher risk of ectopic pregnancy among women who have had one or more abortions. Yet the authors of an American study that uncovered a 160 per cent increased risk arrived at the strange conclusion that abortion "does not carry a large excess risk" of ectopic pregnancy. This is one of many examples in the literature of abortion researchers making statements in the abstracts or conclusions of their articles that flatly contradict their findings.

PID and Other Risks

Uterine perforations, pelvic inflammatory disease, and infertility. Among the other risks involved in surgical abortion are uterine perforation, uterine adhesions, retained fetal fragments and infections that lead to pelvic inflammatory disease (PID). PID is now epidemic in Canada and much of the rest of the world. Nearly 100,000 women contract it each year in Canada alone. The disease is difficult and expensive to treat, and causes infertility in women. The link between PID and abortion is well established in the sense that women who undergo surgical abortions suffer a much higher incidence of PID afterwards. The link is even stronger among women who have had two or more abortions.

Pain and abortion. Some abortion clinics attempt to reassure their patients that the pain they are about to suffer will resemble nothing greater than heavy menstrual cramps. A large study conducted in Montreal paints a different picture. Pain is the most subjective of experiences, yet when the pain scores of these abortion patients were checked against other acute and chronic pain syndromes, "they were found to be higher than fractures, sprains, neuralgia or arthritis, and equal to those of amputees experiencing phantom limb pain and patients with cancer." When it comes to mental pain, abortion is often touted as bringing relief from the depression caused by pregnancy. Not necessarily so. The Montreal study found that 50 per cent of the women who had high depression scores "remained clinically depressed and anxious two weeks after the procedure."

Chemical abortions. Chemical or drug-induced abortions have been hailed in some quarters as a less traumatic solution to an unwanted pregnancy than surgical abortion. Yet these are not without their own difficulties. A variety of studies have found failure rates ranging from 6 to 45 per cent, necessitating a second, surgical abortion. There are unpleasant side effects, including prolonged bleeding, diarrhea, fevers and nausea, as well as the inconvenience of several visits to the doctor and the lack of immediate confirmation of the success of the procedure. Typically, the abortion is not triggered until twenty-four days after the drug has been administered. Furthermore, the pain is reported to be even greater than surgical abortion.

Risks to future children. The most recent studies point to an approximately 85 per cent increase in premature (or "very preterm," meaning less than 33 weeks' gestation) births to women who have had a previous induced abortion. This risk increases sharply with every additional abortion that a woman undergoes. Premature infants suffer a very high incidence of disability. Their rate of cerebral palsy for example, is thirty-eight times greater than that of the general population. Induced abortion, therefore, has appalling implications for women who subsequently wish to bear a child. It is the direct cause of many thousands more cases of cerebral palsy in North America than otherwise would have occurred. . . .

Covering Up the Bad News

Much post-abortion research is conducted by those committed to preserving unrestricted access to induced abortion. Their tendency is to cite only the work of those who share their political outlook on the question. Most post-abortion research is short-term, with the result that long-term consequences tend to be ignored. Many women, especially those who abort late in pregnancy, are unwilling to participate in follow-up studies. Finally, in North America, unlike in European and other countries, there is a pronounced bias against reporting bad news about induced abortion.

In a surprising number of North American studies data on abortion are downplayed or omitted from the discussion or conclusion sections of the paper. Here are a few examples from the highly contentious field of breast cancer and abortion. In 1995 Lipworth and colleagues found that there was a 100 per cent increased risk of breast cancer for women whose first pregnancy ended in abortion. In the discussion section the author downplayed this increase as "at most statistically marginal." In another study Ewertz and Duffy found that induced abortions were associated with an almost fourfold increased risk of breast cancer. In the discussion section this finding was not commented upon, the authors confining themselves to the observation that "pregnancies must go to term to exert a protective effect against breast cancer." A study by Daling and colleagues found a 2.5 risk—in other words a 150 per cent increase in the risk of breast cancer for women whose first pregnancy was aborted before age eighteen—but in their Discussion Section said that their findings "give only slight support to the hypothesis that there is an increase in breast cancer incidence among women of reproductive age."

The investigation of abortion's after-effects is also bedeviled by coding and diagnostic problems. International Disease Classification codes prevent cross-referencing between ectopic pregnancy and induced abortion, even though a clear link has been demonstrated. Pelvic inflammatory disease or Asherman's Syndrome (intra-uterine adhesions, a complication of surgical curettage) may arise from an abortion but not be identified in that way either.

All the adverse effects of abortion put together affect perhaps twenty per cent of the women who undergo the procedure. Though a minority, they are a substantial one. The question that *Women's Health After Abortion* raises is: Are women entitled to know about the risks? Or are those who draw attention to them merely sowing unnecessary despondency and alarm, as some would claim? Fortunately the courts have already established that informed consent must be an essential ingredient of good patient care. Elective procedures—and induced abortion is an elective procedure—require from the physician a greater degree of disclosure than emergency procedures. Common but minor risks must be disclosed. Extremely rare risks must also be disclosed if they have serious or fatal consequences.

The Right to Make an Informed Choice

I co-authored this study because of a conviction that the increased risks associated with induced abortion—breast cancer, death, sterility, ectopic pregnancy, pelvic inflammatory disease, emotional distress, harm to subsequent children, the impact on partners and other children—are serious enough to merit dissemination beyond the pages of professional journals. If women have the right to choose, surely they also have the right to make their choice an informed one.

"Spurious claims that abortion is dangerous should not be used to justify more restrictions on access to abortion."

Abortion Is Safe

NARAL Pro-Choice America

NARAL Pro-Choice America is a national advocacy organization that promotes personal privacy and a woman's right to choose abortion. In the following viewpoint the organization denies that legal abortion is harmful to women's health. According to NARAL, claims that abortion is linked to psychological problems, future pregnancy complications, and breast cancer are unsubstantiated. NARAL contends that laws prohibiting or restricting access to legal abortion are far more harmful to women's health than is abortion because they cause women to delay the procedure, carry unwanted pregnancies to term, or seek unsafe, illegal abortions.

As you read, consider the following questions:
1. How many deaths per 100,000 legal abortion procedures were there in 1973 as opposed to 1997, according to NARAL?
2. What was the conclusion of a large study published in the *New England Journal of Medicine* on the link between abortion and breast cancer, as quoted in the viewpoint?
3. How many times higher is the mortality rate associated with childbirth than that associated with legal abortion, according to NARAL?

As part of their strategy to make abortion illegal and un-available, anti-choice forces are making unsubstantiated claims that *legal* abortion is harmful to women's health. The fact is that the decriminalization of abortion in the United States in 1973 has led to tremendous gains in protecting women's health. The Institute of Medicine of the National Academy of Sciences declared in its first major study of abortion in 1975 that "legislation and practices that permit women to obtain abortions in proper medical surroundings will lead to fewer deaths and a lower rate of medical compli-cations than [will] restrictive legislation and practices." In the years since *Roe* was decided, thousands of American women's lives have been saved by access to legal abortion. Nonetheless, *Roe v. Wade* and the availability of legal abor-tion, as well as the progress women have achieved based on reproductive freedom, are under attack.

Mandatory waiting periods, biased counseling require-ments, restrictions on young women's access, costly regula-tions, and limited public funding have had a cumulative im-pact, making it increasingly difficult for women to obtain safe abortions. Aggravating the problem, the number of abortion providers is steadily decreasing; anti-choice forces have cre-ated an atmosphere of intense intimidation and violence that deters physicians from entering the field and has caused oth-ers to stop providing abortion services. Ironically, many of those now raising alarms about the supposed dangers of abortion are the very persons whose public policy sugges-tions would make exercising reproductive rights more haz-ardous. In pushing for bans on abortion procedures, they re-ject exceptions to protect a woman's health. They seek to restrict access to mifepristone (RU 486), a safe early option for nonsurgical abortion. They deny public funding for abor-tions even when continuing the pregnancy would endanger a woman's health. They put up roadblocks for young women, like the so-called Child Custody Protection Act, which jeop-ardizes young women's health and can force women to have later-term abortions. With these restrictions in place, women's reproductive health is seriously threatened.

The legalization of abortion in the United States led to the near elimination of deaths from the procedure. Between 1973

KalamazooVALLEY
LIBRARIES

Kalamazoo Valley Community College
Texas Township Campus Library

Title: Abortion : opposing viewpoints /

ID: 32972001602004
Due: Wednesday, April 04, 2018

Total items: 1
Wednesday, March 14, 2018 11:47:37
AM
Checked out: 1

Reminders and notices are e-mailed to

your KVCC e-mail address. Overdue
fines are assessed for late returns.
Please renew or return your items by
the due date. Thank you!

TTC Library Circulation: 269-488-4724

and 1997, the number of deaths per 100,000 legal abortion procedures declined from 4.1 to 0.6. The American Medical Association's Council on Scientific Affairs credits the shift from illegal to legal abortions as an important factor in the decline of the abortion-related death rate after *Roe v. Wade.*

Eighty-eight percent of abortions are performed before the end of the first trimester of pregnancy, and 98 percent occur during the first 20 weeks. Earlier abortions are associated with fewer mortality and morbidity risks.

Legal abortion entails half the risk of death involved in a tonsillectomy and one-hundredth the risk of death involved in an appendectomy. The risk of death from abortion is lower than that from a shot of penicillin.

A 1999 study of abortion worldwide found that abortion-related deaths are rare in countries where the procedure is legal, accessible, and performed early in pregnancy by skilled providers.

The Safety of Mifepristone. On September 28, 2000, the Food and Drug Administration (FDA) approved the drug mifepristone (originally known as RU 486) for the termination of very early pregnancy. Mifepristone, which is distributed under the brand name Mifeprex®, is approved for use during the first seven weeks after the first day of a woman's last menstrual period. Mifepristone does not require an invasive procedure or surgery, and requires no anesthesia.

- Mifepristone has been used safely and effectively in several European countries for over a decade, and is now available to women in 29 countries.
- Mifeprex® is extremely safe. Side effects are similar to the complications of a natural miscarriage, and in the unusual case that the abortion is incomplete, the very safe and common procedure of a surgical abortion is recommended to complete the abortion.
- Serious side effects with mifepristone are quite rare. The drug has been used by more than 200,000 women in the United States and has proved safe and effective. Its safety record is much better than many other drugs or procedures.

The Post-Abortion Trauma Myth. In 1987, President [Ronald] Reagan promised anti-choice leaders a report on the health effects of abortion. During the next two years, Surgeon General C. Everett Koop and his staff reviewed hundreds of studies and met with numerous experts in the field. Dr. Koop found that women who have had an abortion are not more likely to experience problems with their physical health, and he was unable to conclude that abortion damages women's mental health. When testifying before Congress, he stated that the development of psychological problems related to abortion is "minuscule from a public health perspective." However, the official report was never released.

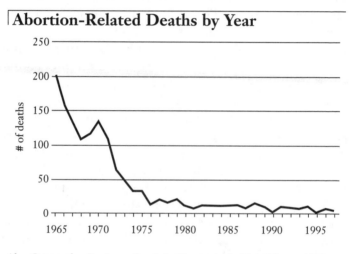

Abortion-Related Deaths by Year

Alan Guttmacher Institute, *Trends in Abortion in the United States, 1973–2000,* January 2003.

An American Psychological Association review found that severe negative psychological reactions to abortion are rare. The review concluded that the vast majority of women experience a mixture of emotions after an abortion, with positive feelings predominating. A 1997 longitudinal study concurred, showing that the experience of abortion has no independent effect on the psychological well-being of a woman. A study published in 2000 revealed that two years after the procedure, 72 percent of the women surveyed were satisfied with their decision to have an abortion, 69 percent said they would have the abortion again, and 72 percent reported more benefit than harm from their abortion. The small proportion of women who did experience problems tended to have a prior history of depression.

The Pregnancy Complications Myth. Medical research incorporating studies from 21 countries demonstrates that abortion does not increase the risk of suffering major pregnancy complications during future pregnancies or deliveries. There is no added risk of infant mortality or of having a low birth weight infant, and the risk of infertility, ectopic pregnancy, and miscarriage following an abortion is not elevated.

The Breast Cancer Myth. Anti-choice forces have attempted to frighten women into believing that abortion causes breast cancer, but no credible research supports this claim. Since 1981, approximately two dozen studies examining the purported link between abortion and breast cancer have been published. The *New England Journal of Medicine* published the largest and most comprehensive of these and concluded that "induced abortions have no overall effect on the risk of breast cancer." In 1999, a study in Denmark analyzed 1.5 million women's records and they "showed absolutely no effect of abortion on breast cancer." Results from a 2000 study published in *Epidemiology* confirmed that there is "no excess risk of breast cancer among women who reported having an induced abortion compared with those who did not, nor did risk increase with increasing number of reported induced abortions." Studies that indicate a link have identified only a slight one—equal to or less than the increased breast cancer risk associated with marital status, place of residence, or religion. In addition, independent experts including the National Breast Cancer Coalition, the American Cancer Society, and the World Health Organization have concluded that a link between abortion and breast cancer has not been established.

Until 2002, the National Institutes of Health (NIH) posted on its website a fact sheet on "Abortion and Breast Cancer" in which it discussed the various studies researching the issue. After a careful analysis of some of the studies, the NIH concluded that there is no overall association between abortion and breast cancer.

On June 7, 2002, 22 anti-choice members of Congress wrote to Department of Health and Human Services Secretary Tommy Thompson complaining that NIH's fact sheet expressed the conclusion that no link between abortion and breast cancer had been established. Soon thereafter, NIH removed its fact sheet from the web. In November 2002, NIH put a revised fact sheet on its website in which NIH, without analysis of the studies, merely stated that the studies are "inconsistent." In December 2002, members of Congress wrote Secretary Thompson to protest the "distort[ion] and suppress[ion] of scientific information for ideological purposes."

After members of Congress protested the change, the National Cancer Institute (NCI) convened a three-day conference to examine the issue. Experts on abortion and breast cancer reviewed all existing information and concluded that "[i]nduced abortion is not associated with an increase in breast cancer risk." The NCI page was updated to reflect this "well-established" conclusion on March 21, 2003.

Illegal Abortion Endangers Women's Health

Women around the world will terminate unintended pregnancies whether or not abortion is legal; the question is whether these abortions will be safe and dignified, or dangerous, humiliating, and terrifying. According to a 1999 study of worldwide abortion trends, approximately 46 million women have abortions each year, 26 million in countries where abortion is legal, and 20 million where it is illegal or restricted. Overall abortion rates for women in developed and developing regions of the world are quite similar (39 and 34 abortions per 1000 women, respectively), even though the legal status of the procedure varies dramatically across these regions.

No exact figures exist of the number of deaths caused by illegal abortions in the United States prior to *Roe v. Wade*. According to one estimate made before 1973, "more than five thousand women may have died [per year] as a direct result [of criminal abortions]. Many deaths from illegal abortion may go unlabeled as such because of careless or casual autopsies and the lack of experience and ability of autopsy surgeons." According to a 1967 study, induced abortion was the most common single cause of maternal mortality in California. Dr. Louise Thomas, a New York City hospital resident during the late 1960s, summed up the dangers of illegal abortion, remembering the "Monday morning abortion lineup" of the pre-*Roe* period:

> What would happen is that the women would get their paychecks on Friday, Friday night they would go to their abortionist and spend their money on the abortion. Saturday they would start being sick and they would drift in on Sunday or Sunday evening, either hemorrhaging or septic, and they would be lined up outside the operating room to be cleaned out Monday morning. There was a lineup of women on stretchers outside the operating room, so you knew if you were an intern or resident, when you came in Monday morning, that was the first thing you were going to do.

In 1966, Romania prohibited the importation of contraceptives and banned abortion for most women. Romania ended the 1980s with the highest recorded maternal mortality rate of any country in Europe—159 deaths per 100,000 live births in 1989. An estimated 87 percent of those deaths were due to illegal and unsafe abortion. A year later, when Romania legalized abortion, the maternal mortality rate decreased to 83 deaths per 100,000 live births, nearly half of its 1989 level.

Each year, an estimated 46 million women worldwide have abortions to end unwanted pregnancies; approximately 20 million of them obtain the procedure illegally. According to the World Health Organization, 78,000 of the approximately 600,000 pregnancy-related deaths occurring annually around the world are associated with unsafe abortion. Where abortion is illegal, the risk of complications and maternal mortality is high. In fact, the abortion-related death rate is hundreds of times higher in developing regions where the procedure is often illegal, than in developed countries.

In 1994, The *New England Journal of Medicine* reported that "serious complications and death from abortion-related infection are almost entirely avoidable. Unfortunately, the prevention of death from abortion remains more a political than a medical problem."

Barriers to Abortion Pose Health Risks to Women

Barriers to abortion endanger women's health by forcing women to delay the procedure, compelling them to carry unwanted pregnancies to term and leading them to seek unsafe and illegal abortions.

Major complications from abortion are more likely to develop the later the abortion takes place. Thus, restrictions on access to abortion and decreases in provider availability—factors that force women to delay abortions—endanger women's health.

- Mandatory waiting periods cause women to have abortions later in pregnancy. A 2000 study of Mississippi's mandatory waiting period law revealed that the proportion of procedures performed later in pregnancy increased after the law went into effect. The proportion of second-trimester abortions rose by 53 percent among women whose closest provider was in-state.
- The American Academy of Pediatrics found that mandatory parental involvement laws "increase the risk of harm to the adolescent by delaying access to appropriate medical care."
- Since 1982, the number of abortion providers has declined by 37 percent. Today, 87 percent of all U.S. counties have no identified abortion provider, and approximately one-third of women of reproductive age live in counties with no provider. The American Medical Association's Council on Scientific Affairs concluded that "mandatory waiting periods, parental or spousal consent and notification statutes, a reduction in the number and geographic availability of abortion providers, and a reduction in the number of physicians who are trained and willing to perform first- and second-trimester abortions increase the gestational age at which the induced pregnancy termination occurs, thereby also increasing the risk associated with the procedure."

Abortion restrictions that succeed in forcing women to carry unintended pregnancies to term expose women to the greater health risks of childbirth.

- The mortality rate associated with childbirth is ten times higher than that associated with legal abortion.
- For adolescents, who account for 20 percent of all abortions, pregnancy and childbirth may entail significant medical problems. Adolescents younger than age 15 are

more likely to experience pregnancy complications, including toxemia, anemia, and prolonged labor. Their maternal death rate is two and one half times greater than that of mothers age 20 to 24, and they are twice as likely to give birth to premature or low birth weight infants.

Barriers to abortion, such as restrictions on public funding and parental involvement laws, may have deadly consequences.

- In 1977, Rosie Jimenez became the first woman known to have died as a result of the federal Hyde Amendment, which restricted funding for abortion except in the case of life endangerment, rape, or incest. Jimenez, a 27-year-old single mother and factory worker who survived on welfare, was unable to afford a safe, legal abortion. In desperation, she obtained a "back alley" abortion and died of complications. After her death, a $700 scholarship check meant to help pay for a college education and teaching credentials was found in her purse.

- The American Medical Association noted that "[b]ecause the need for privacy may be compelling, minors may be driven to desperate measures to maintain the confidentiality of their pregnancies. They may run away from home, obtain a 'back alley' abortion, or resort to self-induced abortion. The desire to maintain secrecy has been one of the leading reasons for illegal abortion deaths since . . . 1973."

- In 1988, a 17-year-old young woman, Becky Bell, became pregnant. When she sought an abortion at a women's health clinic, she was told that under Indiana law, she first had to obtain the consent of one parent. Afraid to disappoint her parents, she had an illegal abortion and died from complications one week later.

Restrictions on Abortion Harm Women's Health

Should anti-choice forces prevail in their efforts, Dr. Thomas' experience in the New York hospital wards during the 1960s, and the deaths of women like Rosie Jimenez and Becky Bell, are events likely to be repeated in the future. Studies show that the more restrictions placed on abortion, the less accessible the medical procedure becomes. However, history demonstrates that restricted access does not eliminate abortion; rather, in an anti-choice climate, women are forced to seek control over their reproductive lives in any way possible, often risking serious injury or death. Liberalizing abortion restrictions reduces the number of clandestine, unsafe abortions. Clearly, removal of legal barriers to abortion would improve women's health, and spurious claims that abortion is dangerous should not be used to justify more restrictions on access to abortion.

"Before she chooses abortion, any woman should be aware of the potential of long-term risks to her emotional health."

Post-Abortion Emotional Problems Harm Women

Valerie Meehan

Valerie Meehan is the editor of *American Feminist* magazine, a publication of Feminists for Life, an anti-abortion women's advocacy organization. In the following viewpoint she maintains that many women who have abortions experience psychiatric problems, including depression and nervous breakdown. She also claims that women who have had abortions have a much higher suicide rate than women who have not. Meehan complains that many mental health professionals refuse to acknowledge this link between abortion and mental health problems. She concludes that women considering abortion should give thought to how emotionally devastating it can be.

As you read, consider the following questions:

1. How much more likely are women who had an abortion to commit suicide versus women who give birth, according to Meehan?
2. According to Meehan, what percentage of women experience lingering depression after abortion?
3. Why is data on abortion's effects hard to obtain, in the author's view?

Thirty years after the [1973] *Roe v. Wade* decision, large-scale research is beginning to find abortion harms women psychologically. But the issue remains clouded by the politics of abortion—and by the shame felt by women who have aborted.

"The whole issue is underground. I had my abortion when I was 16 years old. I didn't deal with it for 19 years. I pretended it was no big deal," says Georgette Forney, chair of the national post-abortion awareness campaign "Silent No More." "One day when I was cleaning out some drawers, I came across a yearbook from that year. I didn't see the kids, I saw my baby. At that point, I came face to face with my pain."

"The shame issue will keep us silent and suffering in silence," says Forney.

Our society wants women to "stuff" their pain, contends therapist Theresa Burke, Ph.D., in a new book, *Forbidden Grief: The Unspoken Pain of Abortion*, written with David Reardon. "As a society we have chosen to tolerate the deaths of unborn children for the purpose of improving the lives of women . . . This moral compromise is disturbed, however, when women speak of their broken hearts after abortion," says Burke.

The increasing number of outreach groups for women who have suffered the trauma of abortion, such as Rachel's Vineyard and abortion rights group The Healing Choice, demonstrates at least some women are seeking therapeutic help after abortion.

Now, several large studies, relying on health and death records of hundreds of thousands of women, have found strong links between abortion and suicide and psychiatric admissions. These record-based surveys, in tandem with a number of smaller studies, support findings of psychological harm.

Abortion and Suicide

Suicide is the most unequivocal gauge of distress. Women who have aborted in the previous year are six times more likely to commit suicide than women giving birth, according to a study based on the health and death records of almost 600,000 women in Finland from 1987 to 1994. Another U.S. study using Medicaid abortion records yielded similar results. Researchers in Great Britain studied hospital admissions for attempted suicide in Wales from 1991 to 1995 and found women who had induced abortions were 225 percent more likely to attempt suicide than women admitted for normal delivery.

In contrast, childbirth seems to protect against suicide. Women who have given birth are half as likely to commit suicide as those in the control groups, according to studies cited in a Canadian book published [in 2002], *Women's Health After Abortion: The Medical and Psychological Evidence*, by Elizabeth Ring-Cassidy and Ian Gentles. The book, published by the deVeber Institute for Bioethics and Social Research in Toronto, Canada, surveys over 500 articles that have appeared in medical and other journals worldwide, mostly during the past 20 years.

Psychiatric admissions jump after abortion, according to several large studies cited by *Women's Health After Abortion*. The rate of hospitalizations for psychiatric problems after abortion is nearly five times higher than for the general population, according to recent research sponsored by the College of Physicians and Surgeons of Ontario, Canada.

The study only concerned itself with a three-month period after abortion, and compared 41,039 women who had induced abortions with a similar number who did not. Another large record-based study of women in California found that, over a four-year period, women who aborted had a 72 percent higher rate of psychiatric admission than women who delivered their babies.

Yet many mental health professionals refuse to acknowledge abortion may underpin a patient's problems, says Burke. The American Psychiatric Association in 1994 removed abortion as a possible "psycho-social stressor" in the fourth revision of its diagnostic manual (*DSM-IV*), the professional bible of the mental health field. In 1992, the prestigious *Journal of the American Medical Association* published a disparaging commentary, "The Myth of Abortion Trauma Syndrome."

Burke quotes a website sponsored by a Planned Parenthood affiliate in Illinois: "You can say or yell 'stop' whenever you have disturbing thoughts . . . If you find yourself fantasizing too often about what the child might have been like,

The Culture of Death and Post-Abortion Depression

We are a society wounded psychologically by the culture of death. Women, in particular, reap disproportionate psychological injury and suffering as a result of health-related practices which are opposed to the culture of life. . . .

When certain practices violate human dignity and the intrinsic nature of womanhood and motherhood, they produce psychological problems based on the denial of the truth about the human person. The more common and yet more subtle area of psychological damage results not as a medical side effect of a particular treatment. Rather, psychological problems can arise as a response to some dehumanizing aspect of the treatment itself. Expressed in other words, psychological problems result not as side effects of medical treatment, but as a result of the health practices themselves. For example, it is a growing practice in obstetrics to recommend abortion when there is a "chance" that the child might be "defective." Or, when a mother is carrying three or four babies as a result of infertility treatments, doctors may recommend killing some of the babies through a procedure euphemistically called "selective reduction." The natural inclination of a mother is to embrace the new life within her and to protect and nurture all of her children, not just some. Instead she is forced to "choose" to kill, supposedly for the good of some of her children or because of the mistaken idea that it is better not to be born than to be born less than perfect. If such actions are contrary to a woman's inherent nature, just what psychological effect can they have?

Researchers in the *American Journal of Obstetrics and Gynecology* showed that the incidence of depression following selective abortion for suspected genetic defect was as high as 92 percent among women and as high as 82 percent among men. The percentage was greater than that usually associated with elective abortion or with delivery of a stillborn. They argued that what was needed was better counseling services to help the parents deal with the guilt expressed.

The culture of death emphasizes psychological counseling to relieve people's guilt. That guilt, however, is the natural manifestation of God's law already inscribed in their hearts. It cannot be counseled away. It must be acknowledged and then it can be forgiven.

Gladys A. Sweeney, "The Psychological Effects: Practices Opposed to the Culture of Life and Women's Health," *At the Podium*, July 10, 2002. www.frc.org.

you should substitute another fantasy: a baby crying because you have no time to give it."

Planned Parenthood, a strong advocate and provider of abortions, acknowledges 10 percent of women will experience lingering depression after abortion, although Planned Parenthood attributes this to pre-existing psychiatric disturbances.

Abortion as an underlying cause of depression is frequently ignored. For example, one young woman, hospitalized for a nervous breakdown, "informed numerous doctors and therapists that her problems began after her abortion. Despite her explanations, no one would consider abortion as a counseling issue. Everyone thoroughly dismissed her abortion as irrelevant," Burke writes.

"They treated me with drugs: tranquilizers, antidepressants and anxiety medication. That's how they handled my grief and pain. They turned me into a zombie," said Kasey (a pseudonym) after her recovery, in an interview published in *Forbidden Grief*.

Teens Are Most at Risk

Ring-Cassidy and Gentles' survey of available literature found that the danger to adolescents from abortion is significantly higher than the danger to adults, according to several small studies. While adolescents are less likely to attempt suicide before an abortion than adult women, they are more than twice as likely as adult women to attempt suicide after abortion, according to a study published in 1998 in the journal *Adolescence*. Meta Uchtman, director of Suicide Anonymous in Cincinnati, reported that in a 35-month period her group had worked with 4,000 women and nearly half previously had an abortion, according to *Forbidden Grief*. Of the 1,800 who had an abortion, 1,400 were between the ages of 15 and 24, Burke notes.

This is particularly significant since abortion is widely seen as a solution to an unwanted pregnancy blighting a young woman's future. One in three abortions in the U.S. is performed on teens.

"A lot of younger girls . . . they've had an abortion on Saturday and they are looking for on-line help on Monday.

They are starting to shut down emotionally, they can't go to school," says Georgette Forney, who counsels via the Internet. "As a 16-year-old, you are not prepared to have yourself violated like that. The trauma totally freaks you out."

Little Objective Research

In general, data on abortion's effects is hard to obtain, with many states collecting no information at all. In addition, researchers are inevitably either pro-life or pro-abortion, although many pro-abortion researchers do not identify themselves as such, Ring-Cassidy and Gentles note.

In 1989, after being directed by President [Ronald] Reagan to study the effects of abortion on women, then-Surgeon General C. Everett Koop stated that all research he found was methodologically flawed. Koop recommended a large-scale study, which was never funded. The survey by Gentles and Ring-Cassidy found the most reliable and extensive studies to be conducted in other countries with liberal abortion laws, particularly in Scandinavia, where extensive records are kept under a national healthcare system.

Very little research has been done using properly matched groups with a control group, the gold standard of scientific studies, Ring-Cassidy says. Many studies consider only short-term outcomes, are often based on questionnaires completed by women shortly after an abortion, and are administered by abortion providers who are biased in favor of a positive outcome, she says. Those reports that look at more long-term follow-up are flawed by "sample attrition," because many women drop out before the study is completed. These women are often most affected by the abortion experience, she says.

While much more research needs to be done, the preponderance of data indicates abortion causes psychological harm to at least some women. Before she chooses abortion, any woman should be aware of the potential of long-term risks to her emotional health.

As Serrin Foster, president of Feminists for Life of America, notes: "Advocating abortion as a simple choice dismisses the huge emotional cost paid by millions of women."

| "*Women experience depression after an abortion in equal or lesser percentages as those women following childbirth.*"

Post-Abortion Emotional Problems Do Not Harm Women

Noy Thrupkaew

Noy Thrupkaew is a freelance journalist and senior correspondent for the *American Prospect*. In the following viewpoint she argues that anti-abortion activists have exaggerated the extent and frequency of the emotional problems that some women experience after having an abortion. Many organizations that profess to offer counseling for victims of "post-abortion syndrome," she writes, really just push pro-life propaganda on vulnerable women. Thrupkaew asserts that there is little evidence to prove the existence of post-abortion syndrome, and she notes that major medical organizations do not recognize the disorder. She maintains that while some women do experience mild depression following an abortion, women who have just given birth experience similar symptoms, with greater frequency.

As you read, consider the following questions:

1. What is a "major stressor" for women who have had abortions, in Thrupkaew's view?
2. According to Rosemary Candelario, why have abortion rights organizations been reluctant to discuss post-abortion emotional problems?

Noy Thrupkaew, "Sick Tactics: The Anti-Abortion Movement Campaigns on Its Latest Ploy," www.prospect.org, January 10, 2002. Copyright © 2002 by *The American Prospect*. Reproduced by permission.

While abortion is perceived by our society as being an acceptable option to giving birth, most women, at some deep level of their being, realize that abortion is an act against nature, and must "shut down" any maternal instincts they may have in order to carry through with an abortion. After the abortion is over, many women are unable to reconcile the fact that they were responsible for the death of their child, and struggle for years with unresolved feelings of guilt and grief.

A woman struggling with negative feelings after an abortion will find that her feelings will not disappear no matter how hard she tries to forget them. Rather, they often lead to a dysfunctional life style. The woman will simply go on with her life never knowing how to overcome the negative, self-destructive behaviors that become a way of life. . . .

—from the website of Silent Voices,
a California-based anti-abortion center

According to Silent Voices, the laundry list of post-abortion syndrome (PAS) symptoms is overwhelming: "Depression, sexual dysfunction, guilt and/or shame, drug and/or alcohol abuse, anorexia/bulimia, suicidal thought." But while PAS advocates argue that a majority of the women who have abortions will suffer these psychological after-effects, reproductive rights activists say PAS is a "nonexistent phenomenon" conjured up by the religious anti-abortion movement. And publicity around the so-called syndrome is the latest weapon conjured by the anti-abortion movement to chip away at reproductive rights.

PAS in Congress

Studies that prove the existence of the syndrome are hopelessly flawed, according to abortion rights advocates; they often rely on data from self-selected subjects who have reported depressive symptoms after an abortion. Neither the American Psychological Association nor the American Psychiatric Association recognize the syndrome. Even the anti-abortion former Surgeon General C. Everett Koop was forced to admit that the risk of serious emotional disturbances post-abortion was "miniscule" after President Ronald Reagan asked Koop to investigate the possible health after-effects of abortion; Koop withheld his findings until 1989.

But PAS nearly gained official recognition from Congress

[in late 2001], before lawmakers axed a measure providing funding to the National Institutes of Health (NIH) to research the syndrome.

New Hampshire Republican Senator Bob Smith tacked Amendment 2085 on to the Department of Labor, Health and Human Services and Education appropriation bill, proposing that the NIH "expand and intensify research and related activities . . . with respect to post-abortion depression and post-abortion psychosis." The measure passed the Senate without debate—the first time PAS has earned any sort of federal recognition—before being scrapped by a House-Senate conference committee.

But PAS is not off the legislative radar screen yet. In August [2001], Representative Joseph Pitts of Pennsylvania drafted a bill that goes even further than the Smith amendment. In addition to seeking research funding, the Post-Abortion Depression Research and Care Act calls for the establishment of a grant program for organizations that provide services to individuals with PAS. The bill is currently under review by House subcommittee.[1]

A Trojan Horse

Reproductive rights activists have argued that PAS is a Trojan horse, an attack on abortion rights cloaked in a disingenuous concern for women's welfare. An examination of the PAS-counseling organizations and their philosophies would seem to confirm their suspicions. According to David C. Reardon, director of the Elliot Institute, which heads the PAS advocacy website AfterAbortion.org, "As we educate [the public] about how abortion hurts women, it changes the whole equation. The potential of post-abortion healing . . . can rapidly change the whole dynamic of the abortion debate in this country. And I am really confident that we will see an end to abortion within the decade."

According to *Ms.* magazine, PAS groups focus on three steps towards "recovery" for women experiencing PAS: confession of the abortion, reconciliation through ritual, and restitution. One example of "reconciliation" is Project Rachel,

1. As of spring 2005, Congress has not passed any legislation recognizing PAS.

which is tied to the Catholic Church, and organizes retreats for "post-aborted women" featuring "rituals, meditations, a memorial service and a Mass of Resurrection." But other organizations go much farther into the "restitution" stage by advising women who have had abortions to actively campaign against abortion.

The Myth of Post-Abortion Syndrome

Since the early 1980s, groups opposed to abortion have attempted to document the existence of "post-abortion syndrome," which they claim has traits similar to post-traumatic stress disorder (PTSD) demonstrated by some war veterans. In 1989, the American Psychological Association (APA) convened a panel of psychologists with extensive experience in this field to review the data. They reported that the studies with the most scientifically rigorous research designs consistently found no trace of "post-abortion syndrome" and furthermore, no such syndrome is scientifically or medically recognized.

The panel concluded that "research with diverse samples, different measures of response, and different times of assessment have come to similar conclusions. The time of greatest distress is likely to be before the abortion. Severe negative reactions after abortions are rare and can best be understood in the framework of coping with normal life stress." While some women may experience sensations of regret, sadness or guilt after an abortion, the overwhelming responses are relief and happiness.

National Abortion Federation, "Post Abortion Issues," www.prochoice.org, 2003.

AfterAbortion.org features model bills, such as The Protection from High Risk and Coerced Abortion Act. The antiabortion Justice Foundation, actually a malpractice firm, encourages women to sue their abortion providers even years after their procedure. Operation Outcry "seeks to overturn the U.S. Supreme Court ruling in *Roe v. Wade* by mobilizing those who have been silent about the harmful effects of abortion. This can be accomplished only through prayer and with the testimonies of women who have suffered harm from abortion." Women who have had abortions, then, become the newest foot soldiers in the anti-abortion battle; Reardon, one of the originators of the PAS movement, calls the women "compelling advocates for the unborn."

Abortion is a difficult choice for many women, and can be accompanied by normal feelings of sadness or regret. However, these emotions do not prove PAS advocates' declaration that abortion hurts women. Depression symptoms after abortion occur for a wide variety of reasons: the stress of an unplanned pregnancy, the breakup of a relationship with boyfriend or tension with parents, and mourning over the fetus. But women are also paralyzed by the stigma of abortion—one that PAS advocates exploit as much as they perpetuate through tactics like "sidewalk counseling" outside of abortion clinics. Lying to relatives and friends out of fear of social disapproval, one study found, became a major stressor for women who had abortions.

Women experience depression after an abortion in equal or lesser percentages as those women following childbirth. For example, less than 20 percent of women who have abortion experience mild, post-operative depression, compared to 70 percent of women who have just given birth, according to Planned Parenthood.

Addressing the potential emotional difficulties of abortion has been a thorny issue for abortion activists as well. As reproductive rights organizer Rosemary Candelario told *Ms.*, "I think the fear in the movement is if we admit abortion is hard for some women, then we're admitting that it's wrong, which is totally not the case."

Attempting to dispel the silence and stigma around abortion, pro-choice organizers have begun implementing more counseling services. The National Abortion Federation runs a hotline that also gives psychotherapist referrals. Many clinics also offer in-house counseling for women after their abortions.

These kinds of services are critical. Abortion opponents have stepped into the silence around the emotional turbulence women may feel after an abortion. Although they have painted themselves as defenders of women's rights, PAS advocates are most adept at co-opting feminist ideas for their anti-abortion agenda. But ordinary counseling provides an invaluable counterbalance, offering women assistance without treating them as pawns in the anti-abortion battle.

Periodical Bibliography

The following articles have been selected to supplement the diverse views presented in this chapter.

Jennifer Baumgardner "The Pro-Choice PR Problem," *Nation*, March 5, 2001.

Jennifer Baumgardner "*Roe* in Rough Waters," *Nation*, February 10, 2003.

Sheryl Blunt "Saving Black Babies," *Christianity Today*, February 2003.

Sarah Blustain "Choice Language," *American Prospect*, December 2004.

Joel Brind "Abortion and Breast Cancer," *National Right to Life News*, September 2003.

Edd Doer "Women's Life, Women's Choices, Women's Voices," *Humanist*, July/August 2004.

Blake D. Dvorak "The Mifeprex Debate Revisited," *Consumers' Research Magazine*, October 2003.

Stan Guthrie "Counter Offensive Launched on RU-486," *Christianity Today*, June 11, 2001.

Bernadine Healy "What Girls Should Know," *U.S. News & World Report*, January 19, 2004.

John W. Kennedy "Complicit Guilt, Explicit Healing: Men Involved in Abortion Are Starting to Find Help," *Christianity Today*, November 2003.

New York Times "Round One for Women's Health," September 13, 2004.

Debra Rosenberg "In *Roe*'s Shadow," *Newsweek*, January 27, 2003.

Amy Sullivan "A Time to Choose," *Washington Monthly*, December 2003.

Pamela Pearson Wong "Abortion's House of Cards," *Family Voice*, January/February 2001.

CHAPTER 3

Should Abortion Rights Be Restricted?

Chapter Preface

Since before the Supreme Court's 1973 decision in *Roe v. Wade*, which legalized abortion, opponents of abortion have argued that the fetus has a "right to life." In April 2004 proponents of fetal rights won a significant legal victory when President George W. Bush signed into law the Unborn Victims of Violence Act.

The law stems from the high-profile Peterson murder trial of 2003. In December 2002, Scott Peterson murdered his wife, Laci Peterson, who was eight months pregnant at the time. In the ensuing trial, prosecutors took advantage of California's law on fetal homicide to charge Scott Peterson with a double murder. (Under California law, only with a double murder charge could Peterson face the death penalty.) Peterson was found guilty of murdering his wife and unborn son in November 2004.

More than two dozen states have fetal homicide laws. However, pro-choice groups oppose such laws on the grounds that they could be used to equate abortion with homicide. The Peterson trial prompted the first federal legislation on the subject. The law established that a defendant may be charged with two federal crimes when an unborn baby is injured or killed during an attack on the pregnant mother.

Supporters of the law deny that it is an attack on abortion rights: "This is not . . . about the most contentious issue of our time and our culture," said Republican House member Mike Pence, "this is about justice." Nevertheless, pro-choice groups have condemned the law. "There is little doubt that it is a thinly veiled attempt to create fetal rights and further erode women's reproductive rights," says Laura W. Murphy of the American Civil Liberties Union. Kate Michelman of NARAL Pro-Choice America says that the law "is part of a larger strategy to establish the embryo with separate distinct rights equal if not greater than the woman."

The fetal rights movement continues to shape the ongoing debate over abortion. The authors in the following viewpoints discuss the laws and court rulings that affect abortion rights.

> "*By making abortion legal nationwide,* Roe
> v. Wade *has had a dramatic impact on the
> health and well-being of American
> women.*"

Abortion Should Be Legal

Rachel Benson Gold

Rachel Benson Gold is the director of policy analysis at the public policy division of the Alan Guttmacher Institute, which advocates for reproductive choice. In the following viewpoint Gold describes how difficult it was for women to obtain legal abortions before the Supreme Court legalized the procedure nationwide in its 1973 decision in *Roe v. Wade*. She writes that poor women had very little access to legal abortion, and more affluent women often had to travel to another state to obtain one. Illegal abortions were common and very dangerous, according to Gold; the number of annual deaths from abortion fell dramatically after *Roe v. Wade*. Gold warns that if *Roe v. Wade* is overturned, poor and disadvantaged women will suffer most.

As you read, consider the following questions:

1. About how many deaths per year were due to illegal abortions in 1965, according to Gold?
2. According to the author, abortion was legal in most states before 1973 under what conditions?
3. How many states does Gold say might prohibit abortion if *Roe v. Wade* is overturned?

Rachel Benson Gold, "Lesson from Before *Roe:* Will Past Be Prologue?" *The Guttmacher Report on Public Policy*, vol. 6, March 2003. Copyright © 2003 by The Alan Guttmacher Institute. Reproduced by permission.

The Supreme Court did not "invent" legal abortion, much less abortion itself, when it handed down its historic *Roe v. Wade* decision in 1973. Abortion, both legal and illegal, had long been part of life in America. Indeed, the legal status of abortion has passed through several distinct phases in American history. Generally permitted at the nation's founding and for several decades thereafter, the procedure was made illegal under most circumstances in most states beginning in the mid-1800s. In the 1960s, states began reforming their strict antiabortion laws, so that when the Supreme Court made abortion legal nationwide, legal abortions were already available in 17 states under a range of circumstances beyond those necessary to save a woman's life.

But regardless of the legal status of abortion, its fundamental underlying cause—unintended pregnancy—has been a continuing reality for American women. In the 1960s, researchers from Princeton University estimated that almost one in three Americans (32%) who wanted no more children were likely to have at least one unintended pregnancy before the end of their childbearing years; more than six in 10 Americans (62%) wanting children at some point in the future were likely to have experienced at least one unintended pregnancy.

While the problem of unintended pregnancy spanned all strata of society, the choices available to women varied before *Roe*. At best, these choices could be demeaning and humiliating, and at worst, they could lead to injury and death. Women with financial means had some, albeit very limited, recourse to a legal abortion; less affluent women, who disproportionately were young and members of minority groups, had few options aside from a dangerous illegal procedure.

Illegal Abortions Were Common

Estimates of the number of illegal abortions in the 1950s and 1960s ranged from 200,000 to 1.2 million per year. One analysis extrapolating from data from North Carolina, concluded that an estimated 829,000 illegal or self-induced abortions occurred in 1967.

One stark indication of the prevalence of illegal abortion was the death toll. In 1930, abortion was listed as the official cause of death for almost 2,700 women—nearly one-fifth (18%) of maternal deaths recorded in that year. The death toll had declined to just under 1,700 by 1940, and to just over 300 by 1950 (most likely because of the introduction of antibiotics in the 1940s, which permitted more effective treatment of the infections that frequently developed after illegal abortion). By 1965, the number of deaths due to illegal abortion had fallen to just under 200, but illegal abortion still accounted for 17% of all deaths attributed to pregnancy and childbirth that year. And these are just the number that were officially reported; the actual number was likely much higher.

If *Roe v. Wade* Is Overturned . . .

The right to choose safe and legal abortion vanishes. Women are hurled backwards into the dark days when women who need access to safe abortion services must once again risk their lives and health to get it. Children whose mothers are not fortunate enough to get an abortion safely will lose their mothers. The woman who bleeds to death from a botched abortion could be your sister, your best friend, your daughter or your favorite aunt. Those who seek abortion and do not die, suffer hideous infections from non-sterile instruments along with the permanent adverse health effects and personal stigma of illegal abortion.

Teenage pregnancy soars. The number of unwanted, abandoned, homeless and hungry children skyrockets. Women and girls who have been raped will have to carry those pregnancies to term. Women who are successful in getting a safe abortion procedure in a doctor's office must consent to permanent sterilization as a condition of the abortion. Those women risk life imprisonment. Women's education, career options and personal freedom are curtailed because they are pregnant for their entire reproductive lives. Women cannot make reproductive choices that are fundamental to their lives and dignity. Only the wealthy can escape with their dignity because they always have, and always will have access to safe abortion.

Karyn Strickler, "When Opponents of Legal Abortion Dream . . . ," *Off Our Backs*, January/February 2004.

Poor women and their families were disproportionately impacted. A study of low-income women in New York City in the 1960s found that almost one in 10 (8%) had ever attempted to terminate a pregnancy by illegal abortion; almost four in 10 (38%) said that a friend, relative or acquaintance had attempted to obtain an abortion. Of the low-income women in that study who said they had had an abortion, eight in 10 (77%) said that they had attempted a self-induced procedure, with only 2% saying that a physician had been involved in any way.

These women paid a steep price for illegal procedures. In 1962 alone, nearly 1,600 women were admitted to Harlem Hospital Center in New York City for incomplete abortions, which was one abortion-related hospital admission for every 42 deliveries at that hospital that year. In 1968, the University of Southern California Los Angeles County Medical Center, another large public facility serving primarily indigent patients, admitted 701 women with septic abortions, one admission for every 14 deliveries.

A clear racial disparity is evident in the data of mortality because of illegal abortion: In New York City in the early 1960s, one in four childbirth-related deaths among white women was due to abortion; in comparison, abortion accounted for one in two childbirth-related deaths among nonwhite and Puerto Rican women.

Even in the early 1970s, when abortion was legal in some states, a legal abortion was simply out of reach for many. Minority women suffered the most: The Centers for Disease Control and Prevention estimates that in 1972 alone, 130,000 women obtained illegal or self-induced procedures, 39 of whom died. Furthermore, from 1972 to 1974, the mortality rate due to illegal abortion for nonwhite women was 12 times that for white women.

Navigating the System

Although legal abortions were largely unavailable until the years just before *Roe*, some women were always able to obtain the necessary approval for an abortion under the requirements of their state law. In most states, until just before 1973, this meant demonstrating that a woman's life would be endangered if she carried her pregnancy to term. In some states, especially between 1967 and 1973, a woman also could receive approval for an abortion if it were deemed necessary to protect her physical or mental health, or if the pregnancy had resulted from rape or incest.

Even so, the process to obtain approval for a legal abortion could be arduous. In many states, it involved securing the approval of a standing hospital committee established specifically to review abortion requests. Either as a matter of state law or hospital policy, these committees frequently required that additional physicians examine the woman to corroborate her own physician's finding that an abortion was necessary to protect her life or physical health. Likewise, a licensed psychiatrist might be required to second the judgment of a woman's doctor that an abortion was necessary on mental health grounds, or a law enforcement officer might be required to certify that the woman had reported being sexually assaulted.

Contemporaneous accounts noted that a woman's ability to navigate this process successfully generally required having a long-standing relationship with a physician. In practice, this meant that the option was only available to those who were able to pay for the review process, in addition to the procedure itself. One study of the 2,775 so-called therapeutic abortions at private, not-for-profit hospitals in New York City between 1951 and 1962 found that 88% were to patients of private physicians, rather than ward patients served by the hospital staff. The abortion to live-birth ratio for white women was five times that of nonwhite women, and 26 times that of Puerto Rican women.

Long-Distance Travel

In the late 1960s, an alternative to obtaining committee approval emerged for women seeking a legal abortion, but once again, only for those with considerable financial resources. In 1967, England liberalized its abortion law to permit any woman to have an abortion with the written consent of two physicians. More than 600 American women made the trip to the United Kingdom during the last three months of 1969 alone; by 1970, package deals (including round-trip airfare, passports, vaccination, transportation to and from the airport and lodging and meals for four days, in addition to the procedure itself) were advertised in the popular media.

Beginning in 1970, four states—Alaska, Hawaii, New York

and Washington—also repealed their antiabortion statutes, and generally allowed licensed physicians to perform abortions on request before fetal viability. Alaska, Hawaii and Washington required a woman seeking an abortion to be a resident of the state for at least 30 days prior to the procedure; New York did not include a residency requirement, which put it on the map as an option for the affluent.

The year before the Supreme Court's decision in *Roe v. Wade*, just over 100,000 women left their own state to obtain a legal abortion in New York City. According to an analysis by The Alan Guttmacher Institute, an estimated 50,000 women traveled more than 500 miles to obtain a legal abortion in New York City; nearly 7,000 women traveled more than 1,000 miles, and some 250 traveled more than 2,000 miles, from places as far as Arizona, Idaho and Nevada.

Data from the New York City Department of Health confirm that this option, as difficult as it was, was really only available to the small proportion of women who were able to pay for the procedure plus the expense of travel and lodging. (Nonresidents were not eligible for either Medicaid-covered care in New York or care from the state's public hospitals.) While eight in 10 nonresidents obtaining abortions in the city between July 1971 and July 1972 were white, seven in 10 city residents who underwent the procedure during that time were nonwhite.

A serious consequence of having to travel long distances to obtain an abortion was the resulting delay in having the procedure performed, which could raise the risk of complications for the woman. No more than 10% of New York City residents who had an abortion in the city in 1972 did so after the 12th week of pregnancy; in contrast, 23% of women from nonneighboring states who had an abortion in New York City did so after the 12th week.

Moreover, a woman who traveled long distances to obtain an abortion not only had to undergo the rigors of travel shortly after a surgical procedure but also was precluded from continuity in her medical care if she needed follow-up services. By the time a complication occurred, an out-of-state woman might already be home, where she would be unable to receive care from the physician who performed the abortion and, perhaps, from any physician with significant abortion experience.

Learning from History

By making abortion legal nationwide, *Roe v. Wade* has had a dramatic impact on the health and well-being of American women. Deaths from abortion have plummeted, and are now a rarity. In addition, women have been able to have abortions earlier in pregnancy when the procedure is safest: The proportion of abortions obtained early in the first trimester has risen from 20% in 1970 to 56% in 1998. These public health accomplishments may now be seriously threatened.

Supporters of legal abortion face the bleakest political landscape in recent history. Congress is poised to pass legislation criminalizing some abortion procedures (termed "partial-birth" abortion)[1] even when they are performed prior to fetal viability and when they are deemed by the physician to be in the best interest of the woman's health; by doing so, the Partial-Birth Abortion Ban Act takes direct aim at the basic principles underlying *Roe*. In the likely event the measure is passed, signed by the president and then challenged, its fate will be decided by a Supreme Court whose balance may have been tipped by the most doggedly antiabortion administration in history. In short, it is more possible than at any time in the past 30 years that the legal status of abortion is about to undergo a major change.

Should the Supreme Court overturn *Roe* and return the fundamental question of abortion's legality to the states, NARAL Pro-Choice America estimates that abortion could be made illegal in 17 states. In that light, the years before *Roe* offer something of a cautionary tale. Granted, it is by no means a given that the precise dimensions of the public health situation that existed before 1973 would reappear. However, it must be considered extremely likely that such an overhaul of U.S. abortion jurisprudence would lead to the reestablishment of a two-tiered system in which options

---

1. In November 2003 President George W. Bush signed into law the Partial Birth Abortion Ban Act, which prohibits abortion procedures in which a living fetus is intentionally killed while partly or completely outside the body of the mother.

available to a woman confronting an unintended pregnancy would be largely determined by her socioeconomic status. Such a system has proved to be deleterious to the health of women, especially those who are disadvantaged, and is something that many had hoped would have been long consigned to the history books.

"Roe v. Wade is . . . characterized by poor logic, poor history, poor social science, and poor jurisprudence."

Abortion Should Be Illegal

Raymond J. Adamek

Raymond J. Adamek is a professor of sociology at Kent State University. In the following viewpoint he argues that the Supreme Court's 1973 decision in *Roe v. Wade* to legalize abortion is flawed. A majority of the public has never supported the decision, he contends. Adamek maintains that the number of women harmed by illegal abortion before 1973 has been exaggerated, and that the number of women harmed by legal abortion since *Roe v. Wade* has been downplayed by the pro-choice movement. Adamek concludes that abortion should be illegal.

As you read, consider the following questions:
1. What is the largest percentage of the public that has ever supported legal abortion "if the woman wants it for any reason," according to Adamek?
2. What three pro-choice myths has the public accepted as truth, in the author's opinion?
3. Why is the right to privacy not absolute, in Adamek's view?

Raymond J. Adamek, "*Roe*'s Days Are Numbered," *Human Life Review*, Fall 2001. Copyright © 2001 by the Human Life Foundation, Inc. Reproduced by permission.

*R*oe v. Wade became the law of the land 29 years ago this January [2002]. Many who were teenagers in 1973 are now sending their own children off to college. Today's young adults, embarking on post-college careers or making wedding plans or counting down nine months to the birth of their own first babies, had yet to be conceived when *Roe* was handed down. Since January 1973, 14 congressional elections have been fought, six presidents have taken the oath of office, and eight of the original nine *Roe* Supreme Court justices have retired. None of this activity has rolled back the decision's broad license to abort. Since January 1973, over 42 million legal abortions have shrunk the numbers of post-'73 generations. Abortion on demand is a right seemingly so firmly entrenched in America that even its most grisly extension, partial-birth abortion, remains legal.[1]

And yet *Roe v. Wade*'s days are numbered (or should be) for a number of reasons.

A House Built on Sand

Roe v. Wade is a house built on sand. It is characterized by poor logic, poor history, poor social science, and poor jurisprudence. So recklessly did the U.S. Supreme Court pursue the unwanted unborn that Justice White, in a dissenting opinion, stated, "I find nothing in the language or history of the Constitution to support the Court's judgment. The Court simply fashions and announces a new constitutional right for pregnant mothers and, with scarcely any reason or authority for its action, invests that right with sufficient substance to override most existing state abortion statutes." Both pro-life and pro-choice lawyers agree that *Roe* was poorly decided.

Moreover, both *Roe v. Wade* and its companion case, *Doe v. Bolton*, were based on self-serving deceptions. "Roe" (Norma McCorvey) was persuaded to believe that her participation in the case would win her an abortion for her current pregnancy, something her lawyers knew was unlikely, if not impossible, given litigation's time frame. She herself initially maintained she was the victim of a gang rape, which was not

---

1. In November 2003 President George W. Bush signed into law the Partial Birth Abortion Ban Act, which prohibits abortion procedures in which a living fetus is intentionally killed while partly or completely outside the body of the mother.

true. "Doe" (Sandra Cano) was not even seeking an abortion, but that is not how her case was presented to the courts. As George McKenna recently pointed out, the pro-choice movement has also been caught in other lies. Sooner or later the public and perhaps even the pro-choice media will begin to appreciate this, and will regard *Roe v. Wade* and its progeny as the illegitimate judicial offspring of lies.

The Majority of the Public Has Never Supported *Roe*'s Policy

A careful reading of public opinion polls reveals that a majority of the public has never endorsed the full license *Roe* gave to render abortion legal for any reason throughout the nine months of pregnancy by whatever method the abortionist chose, including partial-birth abortion. The National Opinion Research Center conducted a series of 17 annual, and more recently biennial, polls from 1977 through 2000 asking, "Please tell me whether or not you think it should be possible for a pregnant woman to obtain a legal abortion if . . ." Among the seven conditions offered respondents is one which reflects *Roe*'s policy, i.e., "If the woman wants it for any reason." The average number of respondents saying "Yes" to this response over the 17 years is 38.5%, and it has never exceeded 45%.

These percentages decrease considerably if we add a time dimension and ask respondents if they think abortion should be permitted in the second and third trimesters as well. Four polls from 1996 through 2000 reveal that while 61–65% agree that abortion should be permitted in the first trimester, this drops to 15–26% in the second trimester, and to only 7–13% in the third trimester. Thirty state legislatures and an average of 61% of the public over 12 national polls favored a ban on partial-birth abortion, a practice upheld by the Supreme Court in *Stenberg v. Carhart*. Thus, while the public does not take a pro-life position on the abortion issue, neither does it support *Roe v. Wade*'s policy.

Why then, in 60 polls taken since 1976, has an average of only 32% of the public supported a Human Life Amendment to overturn *Roe*? Clarke D. Forsythe argues that the public, though not really supporting *Roe*, nevertheless accepts abortion as a necessary evil. The public has largely accepted several pro-choice myths: 1) legal abortion simply replaced one million annual illegal abortions; 2) thousands of women died each year from illegal abortions, and would do so again if abortion were outlawed; 3) legal abortion means safe abortions, which benefit women. Thus, "However bad Americans feel about abortion, [they believe] legal prohibitions would only make the problem worse."

Research Data Explodes Myths

Each of these myths has been exploded by research and hard data, some of which emerged only after many years' experience of abortion-on-demand.

1) In a detailed analysis, Cynthia McKnight has shown that the oft-cited "one million illegal abortions" is simply a "guesstimate" based on questionable extrapolations from a few small or unrepresentative sample studies going back to the early 1900s. As sometimes happens, the one million figure becomes "truth" through repetition. McKnight also reviews a study based on government figures for the number of live births and material deaths due to pregnancy and abortion in the 32 years prior to *Roe v. Wade*. She concludes, with the study's authors, that the average number of illegal abortions occurring annually during this period was 98,000. Although tragic, this number is less than one-tenth of the one million illegal abortions claimed by pro-choice advocates, and less than one-thirteenth of the 1.3 million annual legal abortions now occurring. Thus, legalizing abortion has caused 13 times as many unborn humans to die, and exposed 13 times as many women to the hazards of abortion annually.

2) According to the National Center for Health Statistics, in 1966, the year before the pro-abortion movement began to have legislative impact in some of the states, 159 women died from illegal abortions, not the "thousands" extravagantly claimed by pro-choicers. In 1972, the year before *Roe* legalized abortion-on-demand throughout the country, 41 women died from illegal abortion.

3) Hence, thousands of women did not die from illegal abortions each year, and neither are thousands likely to do so, if most abortions are made illegal again. Poland's experience may be instructive here. Dr. Jack Willke has reported

that under Communist rule in Poland, where abortion was not only legal but paid for by the government, 168,600 abortions occurred in 1965, a peak year. Sixty thousand abortions occurred in 1990. In 1993, after Communist rule ended, the Polish parliament outlawed abortion except for rape, incest, or to save the mother's life. What happened? Did more women die from illegal abortions? Did child health suffer as the result of increased, botched abortions? No, maternal deaths decreased from 70 in 1990 to 21 in 1996 and miscarriages decreased by 25% between 1990 and 1997. Neonatal deaths decreased from 19 per 1000 births in 1990 to 9.6 per 1000 in 1998. Whatever the combination of causes for these improvements, clearly neither women nor babies were worse off without abortion-on-demand.

4) Accumulating evidence indicates that legal abortion harms women. A brief review of some of this evidence follows.

Maternal Deaths. Pro-choice advocates suggest that legal abortion is many times safer for the woman than childbirth. The U.S. Centers for Disease Control report that the maternal death rate for legal abortions fell from 4.1 per 100,000 in 1973 to 0.8 per 100,000 in 1991, the last date for which figures are available. The CDC also reports that 263 women died from legal abortions between 1973 and 1991, an average of 14 a year. However, some authors maintain that this is a vast undercount. Kevin Sherlock, an investigative reporter who examined newspaper articles and public records in county courthouses, coroner's offices, and morgues, found 30–40% more abortion-related maternal deaths across the country during 1980–1989 than reported by the CDC. Sherlock also reported that a memo to local abortion clinics from Dr. Steven C. Joseph, the Health Commissioner for New York City, identified 30 maternal deaths during 1981–1984 in that city alone, at the same time that CDC reports were showing only 42 abortion-related deaths for the entire nation. Dr. Joseph's memo also referred to unpublished data that revealed there were 176 maternal deaths nationwide during 1981–1984, a figure 419% higher than the CDC numbers.

The abortion debate has politicized medicine itself. Mark Crutcher, author of *Lime 5*, points out that although abortion is the most frequent operation in the United States, relatively little data on abortion complications are gathered by the CDC, and the data we have come in very slowly. Crutcher also reports that at the time he investigated the CDC, 50% of their 68 upper-level employees had ties to pro-choice organizations, including 17 CDC doctors who themselves performed abortions. . . .

Abortion Should Be Outlawed

Because abortion is the taking of an innocent human life, it should be outlawed by the government, whose main duty is to protect the common good and thus the fundamental right to life, from conception/fertilization until natural death.

That should be the main message of the pro-life movement.

Matt C. Abbott, *The Wanderer*, September 25, 2003.

[Many studies] strongly indicate that legal abortion is neither safe nor beneficial for women. As the public begins to become aware of the extent to which it has been deceived by the pro-choice movement, it will be more favorably disposed to changing *Roe v. Wade's* policy.

How Will *Roe v. Wade* Be Changed?

Whether the abortion policy flowing from *Roe* changes as a result of a Federalism Amendment, a Human Life Amendment, or some other process remains to be seen. It may not be necessary to pass either of these types of amendments. Paradoxically, the policies now resulting from *Roe* may be changed by applying some of the dictates of that decision itself. Recall that *Roe v. Wade* based a woman's right to abortion on three main reasons:

1) Although "The Constitution does not explicitly mention any right of privacy," its roots may be found in one or more of five Amendments, and "in the penumbras of the Bill of Rights . . . This right of privacy . . . is broad enough to encompass a woman's decision whether or not to terminate her pregnancy."

2) In contrast to the manner in which it discovered the unmentioned right of privacy, the Court noted that "The Constitution does not define 'person' in so many words" and "in nearly all" cases where that word is used, "it has applica-

tion only postnatally." Hence, it concluded the unborn are *not* protected as persons by the Constitution.

3) Based on a now discredited analysis by Cyril Means, the Court accepted the proposition that early laws prohibiting abortion were motivated "solely to protect the woman," and not by a concern for the lives of the unborn. It therefore concluded that, at least in the first trimester, since legal abortion was now allegedly as safe as or safer than normal childbirth, "any interest of the State in protecting the woman from an inherently hazardous procedure . . . has largely disappeared."

However, in four places in the body of its decision, the Court also noted that the State had a legitimate interest in protecting women's health; this permitted the State to regulate abortion. In 1973, relying on the medical evidence it accepted, and focusing on abortion's immediate health impact, the Court thought that this State interest became operative in the second trimester and beyond. It further determined that the State's interests in "safeguarding health, in maintaining medical standards, and in protecting potential life . . . become sufficiently compelling to sustain regulation of the factors that govern the abortion decision. The privacy right involved, therefore, cannot be said to be absolute." Moreover, the Court noted that lower courts have agreed that the right of privacy is "not absolute and is subject to some limitations; and that at some point the state interests as to protection of health, medical standards, and prenatal life, become dominant. We agree with this approach."

Up until now, the Court's pro-choice majorities have contradicted its own statements in *Roe* by treating the woman's right to privacy as absolute, and by preventing any legislative or administrative attempts to protect prenatal life in any meaningful way. However, it is not inconceivable that future, more pro-life Courts could respond to the long-term threats to women's life and health noted above by using these same passages in *Roe* to permit the State to curtail (or perhaps even outlaw) abortion. As Robert M. Byrn noted in his analysis of the "perversion of privacy," "Judges are not deaf to the voices of reason, history and public outrage." Such outrage could well emanate once enough people realize that the Court's pro-abortion decisions and activities of the pro-choice movement have been grounded on deceptions that jeopardize women's lives and health. Together with more effective communication of the pro-life message, this public outrage could help initiate the culture change necessary to support pro-life policies far into the future.

Awakening the Public

Because *Roe v. Wade* is a house built on sand, because the pro-choice movement has been deceptive, because a majority of the public has never supported the policies flowing from *Roe*, and because legal abortion has proven harmful to women both in the short term and the long term, *Roe v. Wade*'s days are, or should be, numbered. . . .

Only a pro-life majority on the Court will overturn *Roe v. Wade* and its progeny, or even follow the rationale of *Roe* by allowing the State to prohibit abortion to protect women's health. Such a majority depends on awakening the public to how we arrived at abortion on demand, and how many unhappy consequences have accumulated in its 29-year wake.

"[Pro-life] legislation has been effective at protecting the unborn and has paid some real dividends."

Access to Abortion Should Be Restricted

Michael J. New

Michael J. New is a research fellow at Harvard University and an assistant professor at the University of Alabama. In the following viewpoint, written in October 2004, he argues that pro-life legislators' efforts to restrict access to abortion have been effective in reducing the number of abortions in their states. New was part of a study that examined abortion data in states with parental-involvement laws (which require a parent to be notified if a teenager has an abortion), Medicare-funding restrictions, informed-consent laws (which require a women to receive information about fetal development and the risks of abortion), and partial-birth abortion bans. The study found that each type of pro-life legislation succeeded in reducing the abortion rate. New concludes that pro-life voters should continue to support these types of laws.

As you read, consider the following questions:
1. How many states had informed-consent laws in 1992 as opposed to 2000, according to New?
2. What type of legislation does the author say had the most impact on abortion rates?
3. What Supreme Court decision does New say gave state legislatures greater authority to regulate abortion?

In recent weeks there has been a flurry of articles by religious leaders arguing that voters should consider issues besides abortion when voting in the 2004 election. Some have even argued that a president who supports abortion rights may better be able to advance the goals of the pro-life movement. In a *New York Times* editorial, Mark Roche—the dean of the College of Arts and Letters at Notre Dame—argues that the abortion rate went down under President [Bill] Clinton, but increased under President [Ronald] Reagan. Dr. Glen Harold Stassen offers a similar argument in *Sojourners*.

Most of these authors attempt to make one of two points: either a) that there is little that elected officials can do to stop abortion through legislation, or b) that the pro-life movement has not reaped any real benefits from supporting candidates who oppose abortion. As such, voters should place greater emphasis on other issues. However, a careful analysis of the data from the 1980s and 1990s indicates that these arguments are flawed. In fact, the success of pro-life candidates has resulted in real reductions in the abortion rate.

State Laws Have Been Effective

For instance, the decline in the abortion rate during the 1990s had virtually nothing to do with policies enacted by President Clinton, and much to do with the sharp increase in pro-life legislation that was enacted at the state level:

- In 1992, virtually no states were enforcing informed-consent laws; by 2000, 27 states had informed-consent laws in effect.
- In 1992, no states had banned or restricted partial-birth abortion; by 2000, twelve states had bans or restrictions in effect.
- In 1992, only 20 states were enforcing parental-involvement statutes; by 2000, 32 states were enforcing these laws.

How do we know that these laws had an impact? A comprehensive study by the Heritage Foundation sheds some light on this important question. The study examines state abortion data for every year from 1985 to 1999. Holding constant a variety of economic and demographic factors, the Heritage study examines the impact of four common types of pro-life legislation: parental-involvement laws, Medicaid-funding restrictions, informed-consent laws, and partial-birth-abortion bans.

Pro-Life Legislation Makes a Difference

Annual abortion totals reached their peak in 1990, topping the 1.6 million mark, but from that point on showed a significant and steady decline. By decade's end, the annual figure was closer to 1.3 million, the lowest in over 20 years.

Abortion rates, which hovered between 23 and 25 abortions per 1,000 women of reproductive age throughout the 1980s, finally dropped to 20 per thousand or fewer by decade's end. The drop in the abortion ratio was even more striking, dropping from 344 abortions/1,000 live births to less than 300/1,000 by 1999. The last time similarly low figures were recorded was 1976. . . .

Pro-life legislation passed during the decade certainly contributed to the decline. Eighteen states passed informed consent or "right to know" laws since 1989, most of them still in effect despite vigorous legal challenges. All told, 24 states have parental involvement laws in effect, requiring either that a minor's parents be notified or that a teen receive her parent's consent to obtain an abortion. Other states have put waiting periods in place. Many of these laws were passed in the early 1990s.

Twenty-seven states passed partial-birth abortion bans in the 20th century's last decade. Congress voted three times to ban the procedure but vetoes and threats of vetoes by pro-abortion President Bill Clinton assured that no partial-birth abortion ban became law. Though the Supreme Court struck down these state bans in June 2000, the debate and passage of these laws was enormously effective in drawing attention to the humanity of the unborn and the inhumanity of those who defend this barbaric procedure.

National Right to Life News, "Abortion Statistics and Trends over the Past Thirty Years," January 2003.

The findings indicate that each of these four types of legislation resulted in reductions in state abortion rates. Restrictions on Medicaid funding of abortions had the largest and most statistically significant impact. The enactment of informed-consent laws resulted in statistically significant reductions as well.

So what generated this increase in pro-life legislation? There are two primary factors and both directly result from the election of pro-life candidates. First, the Supreme Court nominees of Presidents Reagan and [George] Bush gave state level pro-life legislation greater legal protection in their *Casey v. Planned Parenthood* decision in 1992.

Many in the right-to-life movement were disappointed that the Supreme Court did not use *Casey* as an opportunity to overturn *Roe v. Wade*. However, in *Casey* the Supreme Court found constitutional some of the policies contained in Pennsylvania's Abortion Control Act. As such, this decision did give pro-life legislators at the state level more freedom to enact laws designed to protect the unborn.

Prior to *Casey*, the only laws that consistently withstood judicial scrutiny were parental-involvement laws and Medicaid-funding restrictions. After *Casey*, informed-consent laws received constitutional protection. Informed-consent laws require women seeking abortions to receive information about fetal development, the health risks involved with obtaining an abortion, and public and private sources of support for single mothers. Furthermore, after *Casey* many state-level partial-birth-abortion bans were upheld as well.

Second, during the 1994 elections, Republicans won control of both chambers of the state legislature in eleven additional states. In most cases, Republicans maintained control of these legislatures through the end of the decade. Since Republicans at both the state and federal level tend to be more supportive of pro-life legislation, this made it easier for pro-lifers to enact protective legislation at the state level. Overall, it seems that political victories by pro-life candidates have made a real difference.

During the past 31 years, the right-to-life movement has worked tirelessly to protect the unborn. Progress has not come as quickly as many of us would like. However, political victories at the federal level in the 1980s and at the state level in the 1990s have made it easier to pass pro-life legislation. This legislation has been effective at protecting the unborn and has paid some real dividends. Furthermore, considering the fact that the next president may have the opportunity to nominate as many as four justices to the Supreme Court, the right-to-life movement would be well advised to stay the course in 2004.

"Attacks on women's reproductive rights are occurring daily."

Access to Abortion Should Not Be Restricted

Georgana Hanson

Georgana Hanson, an associate with the Reproductive Health Technologies Project, is a long-standing advocate of women's reproductive rights. She has worked with the National Women's Health Network, the Abortion Access Project, and the National Abortion Federation. In the following viewpoint, written in fall 2003, she warns that anti-abortion advocates are continuously working to restrict women's access to abortion. Hanson criticizes laws that force women to undergo counseling before receiving an abortion, require minors to obtain consent from their parents before they can get an abortion, impose unnecessary regulatory requirements on abortion providers, and provide legal protections to the fetus. All of these laws, warns Hanson, are part of a broader campaign to destroy women's reproductive freedom.

As you read, consider the following questions:

1. What type of information is often given to women under informed consent laws, in Hanson's opinion?
2. What are TRAP laws, as described by Hanson?
3. What is the covert intention of laws that give rights to the fetus, in the author's view?

Georgana Hanson, "State by State, Chipping Away at Reproductive Rights," *Network News*, vol. 28, September/October 2003, pp. 4–6. Copyright © 2003 by the National Women's Health Network. Reproduced by permission.

January 22 [2003] marked the 30th anniversary of the Supreme Court's groundbreaking ruling that women have a fundamental and constitutional right to assert control over their reproductive health. "Motherhood by choice, not chance" was the cry of women in 1973, and unfortunately the fears behind that cry remain valid 30 years later. The past decade has seen the steady erosion of women's reproductive rights as anti-choice advocates and lawmakers at the state and federal levels continue to create and enact legislation impeding women's access to abortion services.

Public focus has centered on federal judicial nominees and the prospect of the retirement of a Supreme Court justice, paving the way for the repeal of *Roe v. Wade*. But pro-choice advocates and groups are more concerned about activities at the state level. Since 1995, states have enacted 335 anti-choice measures, creating a patchwork of restrictions affecting women throughout the U.S. The following is a snapshot of a few types of anti-choice legislation being enacted at the state level. Our hope is that after reading this article, you become as concerned and outraged as we are, and that you use that energy to battle anti-choice forces in your state.

Mandatory Delays and Biased Counseling: 20 States

Anti-choice lawmakers in 20 states have enacted laws that force women to delay abortions as long as 48 hours after receiving state-mandated counseling. Erroneously entitled "informed consent" or "women's right to know" laws, these often give women medically inaccurate and misleading information in the hopes that they will reverse their decision to terminate the pregnancy. The majority of the states that have enacted and now enforce such laws require women to visit their provider on two separate occasions, one to receive the mandated counseling and again for the procedure. The extra visit creates a substantial burden for young women, low-income women and women who live in rural areas by subjecting them to increased travel time and costs, the need to take additional time off from work or school, and/or the necessity of arranging for child care. These laws not only obstruct women from getting the care they need, but they also insinuate that women are unable to make informed and responsible decisions for themselves.

- On June 20, Governor Rick Perry of Texas signed into law a bill that would require women to wait 24 hours before obtaining an abortion. The law also requires physicians to explore alternatives to having an abortion, discuss with the women the medical risks associated with the procedure, and show the patients color pictures of the developing fetus. In a state where 93 percent of countries lack an abortion provider, this law only hurts women by forcing them to surpass considerable barriers to receive the care they need and deserve.

Parental Consent/Notification Laws: 33 States

In an effort to "protect our youth," state lawmakers have enacted legislation requiring minor women to involve their families in decisions regarding the women's reproductive health. Some require the minor to obtain consent from a parent; others require physicians to notify minors' parents of the women's intent to terminate a pregnancy. While we all aspire to live in a world where families are caring, understanding and supportive of one another, the reality is often far bleaker. Some young women live in abusive homes, some parents are anti-choice and the list continues. In a supposed effort to amend this issue, lawmakers have created a judicial bypass system that lets minors who cannot notify or receive the consent of their parents seek permission to terminate through a judge. Clearly, revealing personal information to a powerful stranger is a potentially terrifying experience that could deter young women from using the judicial bypass system. Also, many judges themselves are anti-choice and will deny women their right to a legal procedure regardless of the circumstances. As of late July, 19 states require parental consent, and 14 require parental notification.

- In June, Governor Craig Benson signed into law New Hampshire's first abortion regulation requiring physicians to notify the parents of minors wishing to terminate a pregnancy. Young women in the state will be able to seek judicial bypass if they do not wish to have their parent(s) involved. The law goes into effect on December 31.

Refusal Clauses: 45 States

Another means of restricting access to abortion services involves letting providers refuse to offer certain services that conflict with their moral or religious views. Such laws are usually termed "refusal" or "conscience clauses" and pertain to hospitals, physicians, pharmacists and insurers. These clauses allow individuals or institutions to deny women counseling services, medical procedures, referrals and insurance coverage if the care the woman is seeking conflicts with the provider's personal views. Refusal clauses can prevent women from receiving medically appropriate care, further endangering their health and well-being. Forty-five states allow individuals and institutions to refuse to provide abortion-related services. Of these, 12 allow refusal of contraceptive services, and 16 allow refusal of sterilization procedures (as does West Virginia, which doesn't allow the broader refusal clauses).

- Aiming to make Wisconsin the 46th state in this category, state legislators there hope to pass a bill that will allow "health care workers" to refuse certain services if they conflict with personal moral and religious beliefs. Such services could include providing abortions and in vitro fertilization. Pharmacists could also refuse to dis-

"Your life is in danger? So what?!
We're only concerned with the sanctity of life!"

Beattie. © 1997 by Copley News Service. Reproduced by permission.

pense any medication they believed would be used as an abortifacient or for euthanasia, even when prescribed by a doctor for other purposes.

Targeted Regulation of Abortion Providers (TRAP) Laws: 24 States

TRAP laws are yet another example of how anti-choice lawmakers single out abortion providers by requiring them to comply with outrageous additional requirements. Disguised as promoting maternal health and safety, TRAP laws often impose various health requirements exclusively upon physicians and facilities that provide abortions, and not upon facilities that do not. Physicians often find that such requirements impose unnecessary financial and regulatory burdens that make it increasingly difficult to offer services. Twenty-four states have TRAP laws that are enforceable and apply to providers of abortion services during the first and/or second trimester. Examples:

- "Health Department inspectors shall have access to all properties and areas, objects, records and reports [of the abortion facility] and shall have the authority to make photocopies of those documents required in the course of inspections or investigations." South Carolina Regulation 61-12 Section 102-F.
- "Abortion procedure and recovery rooms shall have a minimum of six air changes per hour. All air supplied to procedure rooms shall be delivered at or near the ceiling and must pass through a minimum of one filter bed with a minimum filter efficiency of 80 percent." North Carolina Admin. Code 3E.0206.
- "All outside areas, grounds and/or adjacent buildings shall be kept free of rubbish, grass and weeds that may serve as a fire hazard or as a haven for insects, rodents and other pests." South Carolina Regulation 61-12 Section 606.

Fetal Rights: 23 States

Undoubtedly one of the most frightening attacks on women's reproductive rights involves the provision of rights to the fetus, in essence providing legal protection upon conception. Anti-choice lawmakers have capitalized on the public outcry over the Laci Peterson case[1] to push legislation that places the rights of the fetus on a par with those of the woman, with the covert intention of dismantling *Roe v. Wade*. Twenty-three states have introduced legislation that seeks to redefine the fetus as a person by criminalizing harm to an embryo or fetus, allowing the fetus to be eligible for SCHIP (State Children's Health Insurance Program), or including embryos and fetuses in wrongful death claims.

- In June, Texas Governor Rick Perry signed into law a bill that defines a fetus as a person, and thus allows charges to be filed on behalf of the fetus if it is terminated via accident or crime. Additionally, families of the fetus can bring civil charges against the person responsible for the death of the fetus.

Stand Up and Speak Out: Voicing Our Support for Reproductive Rights

Attacks on women's reproductive rights are occurring daily. State governments are all too eager to infringe upon women's rights by creating insurmountable barriers, leaving women unable to access the appropriate care they need and deserve. We must not remain silent. Keep abreast of what state legislators are proposing and let them know that as a pro-choice constituent, you will not continue to support any lawmaker that proposes or supports anti-choice legislation. As election time draws near, campaign for pro-choice legislators and ask that they ensure that your state respects and promotes the reproductive rights of its female constituents. Lastly, support pro-choice organizations that are dedicated to ensuring women's reproductive freedom. Without their constant vigilance, we face an almost certain return to the days of more unintended pregnancies, illegal abortions and women's deaths.

1. Laci Peterson was murdered, while pregnant, by her husband.

| "*Why should Congress and the president limit the few partial-birth abortions that are done? Simply because it is the right thing to do.*"

Partial-Birth Abortions Should Be Illegal

Hanes Swingle

Hanes Swingle is a pediatric physician at the University of Iowa in Iowa City. In the following viewpoint he describes his experiences with standard and partial-birth abortions, detailing how, in the latter procedure, the fetus's head is pierced with a long metal object, then suction is applied so that the head collapses on itself. Swingle writes that many of the fetuses who are aborted late in pregnancy would survive if given proper care. He asserts that late-term abortion is violent and unethical and should be banned.

Editor's note: The following viewpoint was written in July 2003. In November 2003 President George W. Bush signed into law the Partial Birth Abortion Ban Act, which prohibits abortion procedures in which a living fetus is intentionally killed while partly or completely outside the body of the mother.

As you read, consider the following questions:
1. At what point in pregnancy do most states prohibit abortions, according to Swingle?
2. In Swingle's opinion, what factor determines whether a fetus is viewed as a baby or not?
3. What euphemisms for abortion does the author list?

In 1976, I was a medical student on my first obstetrical-gynecological clinical rotation. In my second week on the gynecology service, I checked the operating room schedule and saw I was to assist with a hysterectomy/TAB. At the operating table, I learned that a hysterectomy/TAB was the surgical procedure where the pregnant uterus is removed. TAB stands for therapeutic abortion; the hysterectomy was for sterilization. I held the retractors as the professor methodically excised the gravid uterus.

I already had assisted on two other hysterectomies, one for endometrial cancer and the other for a benign tumor. I had been taught during those first two cases to "always open the uterus and examine the contents" before sending the specimen to pathology. So, after the professor removed the uterus, I asked him if he wanted me to open it, eager to show him I already knew standard procedure. He replied, "No, because the fetus might be alive and then we would be faced with an ethical dilemma."

A couple of weeks later, now on the obstetrical service, I retrieved a bag of IV fluid that the resident physician had requested. The IV fluids were to administer prostaglandin, a drug that simply induces the uterus to contract and expel. The patient made little eye contact with us. A few hours later, I saw the aborted fetus moving its legs and gasping in a bedpan, which was then covered with a drape.

Several years later, I had my only experience with a partial birth, or late term, abortion during my neonatology training.

A Grisly Procedure

One day, the obstetrical resident who was rotating through the neonatal intensive care unit (NICU) was excited that he was going to get to learn a new procedure, a type of abortion. This obstetrical resident explained to several of the pediatric residents and me that a woman in labor and delivery in her late third trimester had a fetus who was breech (a baby positioned buttocks, not head, first) and also was severely hydrocephalic.

The resident described how he was going to deliver the body of the baby and then, while the head was entrapped, insert a trochar (a long metal instrument with a sharp point) through the base of the skull. During the final portion of this procedure, he indicated that he would move a suction catheter back and forth across the brainstem to ensure that the baby would be born dead.

Several of the pediatric residents kept saying, "You're kidding" and "You're making this up," in disbelief. The pediatric residents all had experience caring for infants and children with hydrocephalus and had been taught that with any one infant the degree of future impairment is difficult, if not impossible, to predict.

Later that afternoon, the obstetrical resident performed the procedure, but unfortunately the infant was born with a heartbeat and some weak gasping respirations, so the baby was brought to the NICU. All live-born infants, even if it is clear that they were going to die in a short period of time, were always brought to the NICU so they could die with dignity, not left in the corner of Labor and Delivery.

I admitted this slightly premature infant, who weighed about 4 pounds or 5 pounds. His head was collapsed on itself. The bed was a mess from blood and drainage. I did my exam (no other anomalies were noted), wrote my admission note, then pronounced the baby dead about an hour later.

Normally, when a child is about to die in the NICU and the parents are not present, one of the staff holds the child. No one held this baby, a fact that I regret to this day. His mother's life was never at risk.

Violent and Unethical

When I was in medical school, abortions were done up until 28 weeks (full term is 40 weeks). It was confusing that on one side of the obstetrical unit, pediatricians were placing extremely premature infants on warmers, intubating them to help them breathe, and rushing them off to the NICU, while on the other side similar premature infants/fetuses were being delivered in bedpans and covered with drapes. Most 28-week fetuses died back then, even with NICU care. Today, more than 95 percent of all 28-week premature infants survive and thrive. Most states won't do an abortion beyond 24 weeks now. However, today more than 50 percent of all 24-week premature infants survive if delivered in a hospital with an NICU, and infants as young as 22 weeks have survived and done well. Infants weighing as little as 9 ounces or 10 ounces have survived.

Excerpts from the Partial Birth Abortion Ban Act of 2003

The Congress finds and declares the following:

(1) A moral, medical, and ethical consensus exists that the practice of performing a partial-birth abortion—an abortion in which a physician delivers an unborn child's body until only the head remains inside the womb, punctures the back of the child's skull with a Sharp instrument, and sucks the child's brains out before completing delivery of the dead infant—is a gruesome and inhumane procedure that is never medically necessary and should be prohibited.

(2) Rather than being an abortion procedure that is embraced by the medical community, particularly among physicians who routinely perform other abortion procedures, partial-birth abortion remains a disfavored procedure that is not only unnecessary to preserve the health of the mother, but in fact poses serious risks to the long-term health of women and in some circumstances their lives. . . .

[14] (L) The gruesome and inhumane nature of the partial-birth abortion procedure and its disturbing similarity to the killing of a newborn infant promotes a complete disregard for infant human life that can only be countered by a prohibition of the procedure. . . .

[14] (O) For these reasons, Congress finds that partial-birth abortion is never medically indicated to preserve the health of the mother; is in fact unrecognized as a valid abortion procedure by the mainstream medical community: poses additional health risks to the mother; blurs the line between abortion and infanticide in the killing of a partially-born child just inches from birth; and confuses the role of the physician in childbirth and should, therefore, be banned.

U.S. Congress, Partial Birth Abortion Ban Act of 2003.

As a neonatologist who has cared for numerous spontaneously aborted and a few intentionally aborted fetuses in the past 20 years, I now realize that the difference between a fetus and a premature infant is a social distinction, not a biologic one.

If it is wanted, it is a baby; if not wanted, it is a fetus. When I started medical school, I viewed abortion as just another medical procedure and the products of conception as tissue. After 20 years of practicing neonatology, I now know this is not the case. I believe that after abortion became legal, the mantra of "it's just tissue" took hold in the medical and lay communities, and most never stopped to question if it were correct.

More than 1.2 million induced abortions are done annually in this country; roughly one out of every four pregnancies is terminated by abortion. Medical or social euphemisms such as TAB, D&C (dilation and curettage), choice, women's health or reproductive freedom don't change the fact that abortion is a violent and unethical—if legal—procedure. Elective abortions have degraded both the medical profession and the women who have made this choice.

Of course, partial-birth or late-term abortions constitute only a minute fraction of the abortions done daily in this country. Why should Congress and the president limit the few partial-birth abortions that are done? Simply because it is the right thing to do.

> "[The federal partial-birth abortion ban] is an extreme measure that sacrifices women's health to further the ideological agenda of the anti-choice movement."

Partial-Birth Abortions Should Be Legal

Simon Heller

Simon Heller acted as the lead trial attorney in the case of *Stenberg v. Carhart*, in which the Supreme Court ruled that a Nebraska law banning partial-birth abortions was unconstitutional. The following viewpoint is excerpted from testimony that Heller gave before Congress in March 2003 on the Partial Birth Abortion Ban Act of 2003 (also known as House Resolution 760). In it, he argues that the proposed federal legislation banning partial-birth abortions is also unconstitutional. Heller maintains that the law does not contain an exception for cases when the mother's health is endangered, and that it limits women's abortion rights in ways clearly prohibited by the Supreme Court. President George W. Bush signed the bill into law in November 2003.

As you read, consider the following questions:

1. For what two reasons did the Supreme Court strike down Nebraska's partial-birth abortion ban, according to Heller?
2. What procedure, banned by H.R. 760, does the author say is in some cases the safest and best abortion technique?
3. According to the author, when constitutional rights are at stake, what branch of government's interpretation of facts takes precedent?

Simon Heller, testimony before the U.S. House Subcommittee on the Constitution, Committee on the Judiciary, Washington, DC, March 25, 2003.

H.R. 760 is not a ban on one clearly defined, late-term abortion method, as its proponents deceptively claim. Instead, it is an extreme measure that sacrifices women's health to further the ideological agenda of the anti-choice movement. It is therefore unconstitutional under controlling Supreme Court precedent. Since *Roe v. Wade* (1973), the Supreme Court has consistently held that the right to privacy under our Constitution gives primacy to the pregnant woman's health: she has the right to end a pregnancy that threatens her health, and she has the right to the safest method of ending the pregnancy. H.R. 760, captioned as a ban on "partial-birth abortion," is unconstitutional in that it suffers from precisely the two flaws identified by the United States Supreme Court in its recent decision striking down Nebraska's ban on "partial-birth abortion." In *Carhart*, the Court invalidated the Nebraska law for "at least two independent reasons":

First, the law lacks any exception "'for the preservation of the . . . health of the mother" [as required by *Planned Parenthood v. Casey* (2000)]. Second, it "imposes an undue burden on a woman's ability" to choose a [dilation and evacuation] abortion, thereby unduly burdening the right to choose abortion itself.

Importantly, Justice [Sandra Day] O'Connor's concurrence re-emphasized these very same constitutional infirmities. The sponsors of the bill seek to evade the *Carhart* ruling in two ways. Neither is successful.

The Ban Imposes an Undue Burden on the Right to Choose Abortion

The Supreme Court found that the language of Nebraska's statute was broad enough to prohibit the dilation and evacuation ["D&E"] method of performing an abortion. Because D&E is the most commonly used method in the second trimester of pregnancy, a law that bans that method is tantamount to a ban on second-trimester abortions. Abortion bans have been unconstitutional since *Roe v. Wade* was decided nearly thirty years ago.

The sponsors of H.R. 760 have altered the definition of "partial-birth abortion," which is not a medical term, but instead a propaganda term designed to inflame public opinion against all abortions. Yet this alteration still does not result in a prohibition on a narrowly circumscribed category of abortion techniques. Instead, just like the language of Nebraska's statute, it could still prohibit many pre-viability abortions using the D&E method, of which the specific technique described in the first paragraph of the bill's findings is simply one type. In fact, the prohibitory language of the bill is quite plainly broader than the abortion technique described in paragraph one of the bill's "findings.". . . The bill perpetuates the problem of Nebraska's law: it uses language which sweeps more broadly than the single technique described in the "findings" by the sponsors.

The Ban Will Harm Women's Health

The sponsors have simply put forward the bald assertion that, contrary to the Supreme Court's holding in *Carhart*, no health exception is necessary in their bill because the technique described in paragraph one the bill's findings is *never* medically necessary and is actually *harmful* to women's health. Both assertions are, however, false. It is thus of little moment that the sponsors seek to label these particular false statements as "Congressional findings." Whatever deference the Judiciary may owe to Congressional findings, no deference is due where the findings are demonstrably false. As Justice [Clarence] Thomas has written:

> We know of no support . . . for the proposition that if the constitutionality of a statute depends in part on the existence of certain facts, a court may not review [Congress's] judgment that the facts exist. If [Congress] could make a statute constitutional simply by "finding" that black is white or freedom, slavery, judicial review would be an elaborate farce. At least since *Marbury v. Madison*, (1803), that has not been the law.

"Medically necessary," in the case of abortion, has two distinct meanings: whether the *abortion itself* is medically necessary, and whether a *particular method* of abortion is medically necessary. The sponsors intentionally conflate the two meanings, even though only the latter meaning is relevant in the case of a ban on abortion methods. Thus, for example, paragraph 14(E) of the findings asserts that the physician "credited with developing the partial-birth abortion procedure" "has never encountered a situation where a partial-birth abortion was medically necessary to achieve the desired outcome . . ." Of course, as with other medical treatments, a pregnant woman and her physician typically choose from among a few alternative techniques to end the pregnancy. But one technique may be *the safest and most medically appropriate* technique. The bill removes the determination of which technique is the safest and most appropriate from the hands of physicians and patients and places it in the hands of federal prosecutors.

A Deceptive Term

Anti-choice extremists have propagated numerous myths about the abortion bans. The new federal statute [banning partial-birth abortions] is part of a deceptive nationwide campaign to eviscerate the key protections guaranteed to American women by [the Supreme Court decisions in] *Roe*, *Casey* and *Carhart*. Contrary to the way its proponents characterized the legislation, its prohibitions are limited neither to one medical procedure nor to post-viability abortions late in pregnancy.

First, despite a deceptive public strategy that has propagated the myth that these bans target a single, specific abortion procedure, the federal ban is not limited to one specific procedure. "Partial-birth abortion" is a fabricated term that anti-choice activists concocted in an attempt to make almost all abortions illegal. There is no medical procedure known as a "partial-birth abortion." Anti-choice extremists created the term as a smoke screen to divert the public's attention away from the true scope of the law, which makes most current second trimester abortions illegal. . . .

The abortion bans are extreme measures promoted by anti-choice politicians and advocacy groups to eliminate a woman's access to the safest methods of abortion. Because the bans are so extreme, medical organizations and the American public oppose them.

Center for Reproductive Rights, "Unconstitutional Assault on the Right to Choose," www.crlp.org, December 2003.

But the Supreme Court has removed this medical determination from the political arena. As the Court stated in *Carhart*, "[we have] made clear that a State may promote but not endanger a woman's health when it regulates the methods of abortion." The sponsors of H.R. 760 assert in their findings that the abortion techniques they are prohibiting are not only "unnecessary to preserve the health of the mother, but in fact pose serious risks to the long-term health of women and in some circumstances, their lives." As is very clear from the factual record not only in the *Carhart* case itself, but in many other cases challenging partial-birth abortion bans, there is, at a minimum, significant evidence that no technique banned by H.R. 760 is harmful to women.

Instead, there is significant evidence that one technique banned by H.R. 760, called dilation and extraction (D&X) by the Supreme Court, is in fact the safest and best abortion technique in some cases. . . .

Perhaps most importantly, the Supreme Court held that the absence of medical consensus about the safety or benefits of a particular abortion technique does not authorize the government to ban the technique: "Where a significant body of medical opinion believes a procedure may bring with it greater safety for some patients and explains the medical reasons supporting that view," neither Congress nor the States may ban the procedure. H.R. 760 directly contravenes this legal holding by choosing one side in the medical debate about abortion methods via the device of Congressional findings. Yet this is a debate the Supreme Court has required the government to stay out of.

The Bill Threatens the Separation of Powers

The bill also presents a greater threat to our constitutional system of government. Where constitutional rights are at stake, the Judiciary conducts its own independent review of the facts. Even where constitutional rights are *not* at stake, the Court has recently viewed with skepticism Congressional findings purportedly supporting its exercise of powers under Article I or Section 5 of the Fourteenth Amendment. Here, the sponsors assert that factual findings made by the Judiciary can be, in essence, set aside by contrary Congressional findings. Under this novel regime, Congress could have overturned *Brown v. Board of Education* by "finding" that racially separate schools were, in fact "equal," or could, in line with this bill's approach, ban all D&E abortions by "finding" that all D&E procedures were unsafe and that, contrary to actual fact, D&E's were rarely performed. Ultimately, Congressional findings that seek to defy the Supreme Court and the function of the federal courts as triers of facts will not only threaten the independence of the Judiciary, but undermine the value of Congressional findings in other contexts where such findings may, unlike in this bill, actually be a legitimate and appropriate exercise of Congressional power. . . .

Congress is attempting to overturn Supreme Court constitutional precedent by enacting a law that fails to adhere to the precedent. . . . Congress has overstepped its bounds—the bill does not pass constitutional muster.

The Supreme Court's decision in *Stenberg v. Carhart* is clear: even a specific, narrowly worded ban on the D&X abortion technique must contain a health exception because significant evidence supports the likelihood that the D&X technique is the safest technique in some cases. *Carhart* also re-affirms that a ban on commonly used abortion methods cannot masquerade as a prohibition on a specific technique, for such a ban imposes an undue burden. This decision is in keeping with the Supreme Court's long-held principle that the health of the pregnant woman must be protected when government regulates abortion, and that government must respect the reasonable medical judgment of physicians and their women patients. Congress would do well to heed the Supreme Court's pronouncement by rejecting this bill.

| "Every day, *international family planning services save lives.*"

The United States Should Fund Legal Abortion in Other Countries

Marty Meehan and Gloria Feldt

U.S. representative Marty Meehan represents the Fifth Congressional District of Massachusetts, and Gloria Feldt is president of the Planned Parenthood Federation of America. In the following viewpoint, written in August 2004, they criticize the U.S. policy of prohibiting any type of monetary assistance to international family planning organizations that provide or counsel about abortion services. This policy, they argue, ensures that anti-abortion organizations receive U.S. financial assistance while pro-choice organizations do not. By reducing the assistance that family planning organizations receive, Meehan and Feldt contend, the United States fails to reduce unintended pregnancies and deaths from unsafe abortions and pregnancy-related causes.

As you read, consider the following questions:
1. How did President George W. Bush expand the Mexico City policy, according to the authors?
2. How many unintended pregnancies occur annually worldwide, according to Meehan and Feldt?
3. What is "A Mother's Promise the World Must Keep," according to the authors?

This week [August 12, 2004] marks the 20th anniversary of a profound and misguided change in US foreign policy: the Reagan administration's "global gag rule," which was first announced at an international family planning conference in Mexico City in August 1984.

The "Mexico City" policy prohibits US dollars and contraceptive supplies from going to any international family planning program that provides abortions or counsels women about their reproductive health options. The policy isn't about money going to pay for abortions. Even those groups that use only private funds for abortion services—where abortion is legal—are barred from assistance. This is money going to family planning programs.

President [Bill] Clinton rescinded the Mexico City policy in 1993. But President [George W.] Bush reinstated and expanded it on his first day in office. Now not only are organizations that provide or counsel about abortion services affected; those that dare to take part in a public discussion about legalizing abortion are also affected (hence the name "global gag rule"). Of course, those that call for restricting abortion rights are not affected.

This policy has nothing to do with government-sponsored abortions overseas. Ten years before the gag rule was in place the law strictly prohibited that. This policy is about disqualifying prochoice organizations from receiving US international family planning funding.

Under Bush's policy, organizations that play a vital role in women's health are forced to make an impossible choice. If they refuse to be "gagged," they lose the funding that enables them to help women and families who are cut off from basic health care and family planning. But if they accept funding, they must accept restrictions that jeopardize the health of the women they serve.

How the Policy Harms Women

The most tragic ramifications have been felt in the developing world. In Kenya, for example, two of the leading family planning organizations have been forced to shut down five clinics dispensing aid from prenatal care and vaccinations to malaria screening and AIDS prevention. Kenya's experience is common, according to "Access Denied," a report on the impact of the global gag rule on developing nations. Researchers found that programs for rural communities and urban slums have been scaled back by as much as 50 percent. As a result more women are turning to unsafe abortion—a leading cause of death for young women in much of Africa—because they lack access to family planning information and essential contraceptive supplies.

Abortion-Related Mortality Rates by Region

Region	Deaths per 100,000 abortions
Developing	**330**
Africa	680
South & Southeast Asia	283
Latin America	119
Developed	**0.2–1.2**

Alan Guttmacher Institute, "Sharing Responsibility: Women, Society & Abortion Worldwide," 1999.

International family planning programs work. For more than 30 years, the United States has supported programs in some of the poorest regions of the world to deliver voluntary family planning and reproductive health services. These programs help educate and empower women to take better care of themselves, their families, and their communities. Every day, international family planning services save lives, reduce the number of unintended pregnancies, combat the scourge of global HIV/AIDS, and promote sustainable development worldwide.

Consider the facts. More than 500,000 women die annually from pregnancy-related causes. Babies of women who die in childbirth are unlikely to survive one year. Family planning can cut maternal mortality rates by 25 percent and infant mortality rates even further.

More than 38 million people live with HIV/AIDS worldwide. Family planning programs provide education and contraceptives that play an important role in curbing the spread of the pandemic.

More than 80 million unintended pregnancies occur annually worldwide, and more than half of them result in abortion (78,000 women die every year from unsafe abortions). Family planning reduces the need for abortion. These are not new issues. A decade ago, the nations of the world came together in Cairo at the International Conference on Population and Development with a unified vision of improving the quality of life for women, families, and the environment. They made a promise to commit moral and financial resources to ensuring that all people have access to information and services that include health care, family planning, and a basic education.

Ideology vs. Public Health

The United States was a leader in that effort. But with the advent of the current global gag rule, this work is threatened. It is the tragic outcome of a decision-making process that puts blind ideology before sound public health practice and global cooperation.

Thousands of Americans have joined together in the campaign "A Mother's Promise the World Must Keep" to call on our government to cooperate with other nations to meet our promise. We must restore common sense and America's leadership role by reversing this misguided policy.

So many lives are at stake. We can't afford to exclude any family planning organization that can safely and effectively provide comprehensive reproductive health services. America should be leading—not gagging—global efforts to improve women's health.

*"The President has rightly removed the
United States from the business of
exporting a culture of death."*

The United States Should Not Fund Abortion in Other Countries

Gail Quinn

In January 2001 President George W. Bush reinstated the Mexico City Policy, which prohibits U.S. funding of any international organization that provides or counsels women about abortion services. Later that year, Congress considered (and ultimately did not pass) two bills, S. 367 and H.R. 755, that aimed to rescind the policy. The following viewpoint is excerpted from a letter that Gail Quinn, executive director of the Secretariat for Pro-Life Activities of the National Conference of Catholic Bishops, wrote to Congress in support of the Mexico City Policy. In it, she argues that most nations, particularly those where abortion is illegal, support the Mexico City Policy because they believe that the United States should not be funding efforts to promote pro-abortion views within their borders.

As you read, consider the following questions:
1. What, in Quinn's view, would S. 367 and H.R. 755 allow international organizations to do?
2. How does the Mexico City Policy help prevent resentment of the United States in other countries, in the author's opinion?
3. What are poor women in other countries calling for, in the author's view?

Gail Quinn, letter to the U.S. Congress, April 18, 2001.

"The poor cry out for justice and equality and we respond with legalized abortion." Thus wrote dissenting commissioner Grace Olivarez, when the Rockefeller Commission on Population and the American Future proposed almost two decades ago that abortion be used to control population and reduce poverty in the United States.

That the mindset of the Rockefeller Commission majority still lives among us is apparent from some reactions to the reinstatement of the "Mexico City Policy" governing U.S. population assistance. Abortion advocacy groups have reacted with outrage, claiming to speak for the women of developing nations who allegedly want help in aborting their children more than any other form of foreign aid.

Because President [George W.] Bush does not believe the U.S. government should subsidize organizations that promote and perform abortions in the Third World, he is accused of seeking to [according to one congressman] "hurt the women of the world." This charge is made by the sponsors of S. 367, a bill designed to rescind the Mexico City policy and give free rein to U.S.-funded organizations to promote abortion abroad.

Under S. 367 and its companion bill, H.R. 755, nongovernmental organizations could attack human life and human dignity and continue to receive U.S. funds, so long as their practices could not be shown to violate the host country's law or U.S. federal law. Population control groups could again distribute abortion kits in nations where abortion is illegal, evading local laws by calling them "menstrual regulation" kits and neglecting to perform pregnancy tests before performing abortions. They could even perform abortions and other "health or medical services" that endanger women, since such abuses may not be adequately addressed by host countries' laws and are seldom addressed by federal law in the U.S. In recent cases in this country involving women's injury or death at the hands of those performing supposedly legal abortions, redress has been entirely through state law. It is tragically ironic that legislation ostensibly designed to prevent "unsafe" abortion may give U.S.-funded organizations new leeway to practice exactly that.

In our view, the Mexico City policy respects the dignity of

poor women in developing nations, as well as the laws and cultures of the vast majority of nations, far better than such gravely misguided legislation does. The President has rightly removed the United States from the business of exporting a culture of death.

Respect for Life and for Other Nations' Sovereignty

About 71% of the population assistance all over the world, as reported by the UN [United Nations], is directed towards countries in Asia and the Pacific (25%), Latin America (13%), sub-Saharan Africa (26%), Western Asia and North Africa (7%). Very few countries where USAID provides population assistance permit abortion under circumstances broader than those allowed under the Mexico City Policy. In addition, abortion is not only illegal in these last countries, but also unconstitutional because the constitution in many of these countries upholds the protection of life since the moment of conception. The Mexico City Policy then is consistent with the desire of most of these countries and with the effort that many countries around the world are making to decrease the number of abortions. Furthermore, it is consistent with the desire of the majority of the population of these countries who in recent years have overwhelmingly opposed any intent, by a minority within those countries, of legalizing abortion. The Mexico City Policy imposes a resonable restriction because it is a job restriction and it is respectful of it as it is consistent with the decision of the population of these countries to uphold the right to life of the unborn child. It is also respectful of the sovereign right of countries to uphold their constitution and domestic laws. Furthermore, the fact that some organizations want to advocate abortion and to perform abortions does not mean that U.S. tax money should pay for it.

Maria Sophia Aguirre, testimony before the Senate Foreign Relations Committee, July 17, 2001.

As the U.S. bishops' Committee for Pro-Life Activities testified in 1989, the Mexico City policy is needed because the agenda of many organizations receiving U.S. population aid has been to "promote abortion as an integral part of family planning—even in developing nations where abortion is against the law . . . Far from being perceived as an imposition on developing nations, the United States policy against funding abortion activity has been greeted by those nations as a welcome reform. The vast majority of these countries have legal policies against abortion, and virtually all forbid the use of abortion as merely another birth control method."

When President Bush reinstated the Mexico City Policy this year [2001], some complained that the policy amounts to "powerful" politicians forcing their policies on powerless women. But as we have learned from our experience in international conferences on population, the promotion of permissive abortion attitudes is much more likely to cause resentment, especially when it is perceived as a means by which the West is attempting to impose population control policies on developing nations as conditions for development assistance.

Poor women in developing nations are not calling for help to abort their children. They are calling for education, food, housing, and medicine for themselves and their children so that they can lead lives of full human dignity. The United States can best respond to their pleas by holding firm to the Mexico City Policy, while increasing true development aid from its scandalous level of one-tenth of one percent of GNP [gross national product], the lowest percentage of all major donor countries. I urge you to reject S. 367 and H.R. 755, and to uphold the Mexico City policy.

Periodical Bibliography

The following articles have been selected to supplement the diverse views presented in this chapter.

Chris Black	"The Partial-Birth Fraud," *American Prospect*, September 24, 2001.
Eleanor Cooney	"The Way It Was," *Mother Jones*, September/October 2004.
Richard M. Doerflinger	"Against Overwhelming Odds: Congressional Efforts and Gain Since *Roe v. Wade*," *National Right to Life News*, January 2003.
Jeffrey Drazen	"Inserting Government Between Patient and Physician," *New England Journal of Medicine*, January 8, 2004.
Economist	"The War That Never Ends—Abortion in America," January 18, 2003.
Cynthia Gorney	"Gambling with Abortion: Why Both Sides Think They Have Everything to Lose," *Harper's Magazine*, November 2004.
Tim Graham	"Pro-Choice Tilt?" *World & I*, October 2003.
Ramesh Ponnuru	"Abortion Now: Thirty Years After *Roe*, a Daunting Landscape," *National Review*, January 27, 2003.
Deborah Rosenberg	"The War over Fetal Rights," *Newsweek*, June 9, 2003.
Roger Simon	"The Argument That Never Ends," *U.S. News & World Report*, January 20, 2003.
Karyn Strickler	"When Opponents of Legal Abortion Dream . . ." *Off Our Backs*, January/February 2004.
Time	"Under the Radar," January 27, 2003.
Sarah Wildman	"Abort Mission," *American Prospect*, January 2004.
Benjamin Wittes	"Letting Go of *Roe*," *Atlantic Monthly*, January/February 2005.

CHAPTER 4

Do Genetic Technologies Destroy Human Life?

Chapter Preface

The rapid pace at which reproductive and genetic technologies are advancing has made the abortion debate more, rather than less, complex. These technologies have enabled scientists to test and manipulate human cells at the earliest stages of development, with far-reaching consequences.

Two of the most controversial technologies are preimplantation genetic diagnosis (PGD) and embryonic stem cell research (ESCR). In PGD embryos are created outside the woman's body and tested for genetic abnormalities or other traits before being implanted in the womb. In ESCR certain cells are taken from embryos that have not been selected for implantation. These embryonic stem cells are able to develop into any type of human tissue, making them valuable for medical research.

Both PGD and ESCR are possible because of the technique of in vitro fertilization (IVF), in which an egg and sperm are combined outside the body to form an embryo, which may later be implanted into the womb. The technique dates back to 1978, when Louise Brown, the first "test-tube baby," was born. IVF is the basis of numerous assisted reproductive techniques for couples trying to conceive.

The main ethical dilemma that arises from IVF is that usually more embryos are created than will be implanted. Those who believe that life begins at conception claim that it is unethical to destroy these "extra" embryos. PGD and ESCR were both developed in response to the phenomenon of excess embryos: In PGD the embryos are tested to select which is most desirable for implantation, and in ESCR the embryos are used to further medical research. Still, both technologies result in some embryos being destroyed, and therefore generate concern among abortion opponents.

It is ironic that IVF—a technique originally developed to help infertile couples conceive a child—has given rise to technologies that, because they result in the destruction of embryos, many people associate with abortion. The authors in the following chapter debate the ethics of both preimplantation genetic diagnosis and embryonic stem cell research.

| *"Using PGD as a method of weeding out undesirable offspring is unethical by its very nature."*

Preimplantation Genetic Diagnosis Destroys Human Life

John F. Kilner

John F. Kilner is president of the Center for Bioethics and Human Dignity. In the following viewpoint he argues that preimplantation genetic diagnosis (PGD), in which "test-tube" babies are genetically screened before being implanted in the womb, is unethical. Parents most often use PGD to select an embryo that is free of genetic disease. Kilner maintains that it is wrong to destroy the embryos that do not meet the PGD selection criteria. He also insists that it is unethical to intentionally create human embryos knowing that many of them will be destroyed.

As you read, consider the following questions:

1. What is the first argument that advocates use to defend "savior sibling" PGD, according to Kilner, and why does he reject it?
2. Using PGD to avoid having a "diseased baby" is a classic example of what, in the author's words?
3. Kilner believes that the money currently being spent on PGD should be used for what more ethical purpose?

On May 5, 2004, a front-page story in newspapers around the U.S. reported the production of babies to provide bone marrow or umbilical cord blood for their sick siblings. The reproduction process involved producing many embryos through *in vitro* fertilization (IVF), testing them for how well they genetically matched their siblings, throwing away the majority who did not match well, and only implanting some of those who remained. The testing technique used in such procedures is called preimplantation genetic diagnosis, or PGD.

Helping sick children is wonderful and should be a high priority. We ache with their parents and are motivated to do all that we can to help. But once we suggest that accomplishing something good can be pursued using any means necessary, we have crossed an ethical line.

Many people are deeply disturbed by PGD. They recognize that beginning new human lives at the embryonic state, testing them to see how useful they will be, and throwing away those who don't measure up is demeaning—and not just to those who are sacrificed. Those who survive are demeaned as well since they are allowed to live only because they are sufficiently useful to someone else.

Some of the worst medical atrocities to date have been rationalized with the notion that there is something wonderful to achieve and no other way to achieve it. . . . We need to be careful lest misguided compassion move us to pursue a quick fix that will foster a way of thinking that will harm a much larger number in the long run.

Why Using PGD to Create "Savior Siblings" Is Wrong

Advocates of the process sometimes defend it with claims beyond the argument that PGD is "necessary." Here are the most common:

1) Some claim that the process avoids the need to abort children later who are not well-matched to their siblings. But, killing developing human beings earlier as opposed to later is no improvement—either way the same human beings die because they don't measure up.

2) Others claim that various risks of the procedure to the

child can be mitigated. They argue that unknown risks to healthy embryos from the genetic testing procedure, and the pressure on children born through this PGD process to donate bone marrow irrespective of their will can be addressed through monitoring and counseling. These are indeed two serious concerns, but the jury is still out on whether the proposed solutions will resolve the issues sufficiently. In the meantime, allowing PGD to go forward constitutes experimentation on children that many find unacceptable. Even if we can resolve these two concerns, other key ethical problems remain.

3) Still others claim that "the public" "supports" the process. Such language seems to suggest virtual unanimity. However, the opinion poll cited in May news reports actually shows the U.S. public divided, with only 60% in favor of the procedure. Furthermore, some countries such as Germany and Italy ban the practice entirely. Regardless, 60% support does not make a process right. If it did, then ethics is nothing more than a determination by the majority's opinion without respect for fundamental truths and rights.

Using PGD as a method of weeding out undesirable offspring is unethical by its very nature. "Savior babies" are just the latest (and perhaps clearest) example of how utilitarian thinking can be demeaning to human beings. Whatever the variation, the basic approach of PGD involves producing many more human beings than are wanted, selecting those deemed best, and discarding the rest.

PGD and Genetic Disease

Most often, the goal is to avoid passing on a genetic disease, though PGD is sometimes used for gender selection or selecting children with other traits as well. Using PGD to avoid having a "diseased baby" is a classic example of identifying a serious human problem and rushing to address it with the most easily accessible method available rather than with a truly ethical technology. Identifying serious problems such as genetic diseases is praiseworthy, and being strongly motivated to avoid them is even more laudable. However, allowing human beings to live only if they "measure up" genetically represents a profound shift in what it means to be a human being. It suggests that some human beings do not have enough value to justify their existence.

Children produced through this technology are received into the world—into a family—only because they do not have some unwanted problem. Their lives would have been terminated if they didn't measure up to being "normal." The demise of unconditional acceptance and love that usually exists when a parent has a child, whether they are healthy or not, does not bode well for the inevitable situations when other unwanted problems arise in a child's life.

It also doesn't bode well for those in our communities who are disabled. After all, if my child wasn't worth saving because of health or disability, why should we tolerate others who intentionally allow a disabled child to be born? Why should we pay for the care necessary to ensure they have as good of a life as they possibly can?

Choosing Which Embryos Will Die

Prenatal genetic testing has reached a new low. On Thursday, June 8, 2001, researchers announced that the first baby was born who had been screened for a disease he may never contract. Doctors at Chicago's Reproductive Genetics Institute performed preimplantation genetic diagnosis on eighteen embryos whose father carried the gene for Li-Fraumeni syndrome, an inherited predisposition to many forms of cancer because of a mutation in a tumor-suppressing gene called P_{53}. Eleven embryos were found to have the gene, seven were determined to be normal. Two normal embryos were implanted in the mother's uterus. One baby boy was born. . . .

So, the life of one child was purchased by the death of seventeen. Seventeen offspring were prevented from having the opportunity to live that the father himself enjoyed.

C. Ben Mitchell, "Silence Is Deadly Business in Genetic Testing," Center for Bioethics and Human Dignity, www.cbhd.org, June 18, 2001.

Embryos are entire beings, not merely cells, and human embryos are, accordingly, human beings. Does every innocent human being have a God-given dignity that warrants respect and protection? Selective PGD says no.

But many people disagree. Some argue that on the scientific basis of genetics, embryos are protectable because they are beings with a full human genetic code. Others would similarly protect human embryos on the biblical basis (Genesis 1) that the image of God is present in living beings who are human as opposed to animal, etc. Still others would protect embryonic humans simply because their status is debatable and uncertain. Just as we take special precautions not to engage in behavior that might harm human beings, they observe, so we should not engage in behavior harmful to those who might be human beings.

The Ethical Use of Technology

Every dollar spent on PGD to identify which embryonic human beings to discard—rather than on developing ethical ways of preventing and curing genetic diseases—is a shame. Compassion for sick children and their families demands a better approach.

Can PGD play any ethical role in a better approach? If so, it would have to involve using it for the good of those tested, rather than employing it to their detriment.

For example, if the purpose is to identify genetic problems in order to prepare for any special supports that will be needed later, then the intention is admirable. However, it is better to avoid the ethical problems associated with producing embryos in the lab, especially if the mother can become pregnant without the use of assisted reproductive technologies. In any case, if future support is the intention, then diagnostic tests other than PGD can be done during the pregnancy to identify genetic problems (although the risks of any diagnostic test must be sufficiently known and limited in order to justify using it to obtain the desired information).

Similarly, if the purpose is to use genetic therapy to correct problems identified through PGD, then the intention is also admirable. But, genetic therapy to correct problems is so undeveloped at the moment that PGD can do little to assist it. Even with developments in genetic therapy, PGD would not be necessary if the therapy can take place later than the embryonic stage, or before conception (with the benefit that the genetic error is corrected in all cells of the body).

Thus the use of PGD would be ethical in a situation

where the use of assisted reproduction technologies is necessary and a genetic therapy is available that must be done at the embryonic stage. But such is never the case today—and some say it may never be.

Then preimplantation genetic diagnosis appears to have a poor prognosis indeed.

> "*When the eight cell embryo is in culture, it has not acquired the additional respect and emotional attachment associated with implantation.*"

Preimplantation Genetic Diagnosis Helps Parents Have Healthy Children

C. Cameron and R. Williamson

C. Cameron and R. Williamson are physicians at the Murdoch Children's Research Institute at the University of Melbourne in Australia. In the following viewpoint they compare preimplantation genetic diagnosis (PGD), in which parents may discard one or more "test-tube" embryos because of genetic abnormalities, to aborting a fetus (in the womb) that is found, through prenatal genetic testing, to have abnormalities. The authors contend that using PGD is ethically preferable because in PGD the embryos are in a less developed state and none has yet been implanted in the womb. They assert that women are not attached to preimplantation fetuses in the same way that they are to those in their womb.

As you read, consider the following questions:

1. In the authors' opinion, given a choice between many possible children, which child should be born?
2. When do most women give an embryo full respect as an individual, according to the authors?
3. What two simultaneous decisions are made in PGD, in Cameron's and Williamson's view?

C. Cameron and R. Williamson, "Is There an Ethical Difference Between Preimplantative Genetic Diagnosis and Abortion?" *Journal of Medical Ethics*, vol. 29, April 2003, pp. 90–92. Copyright © 2003 by the British Medical Association. Reproduced by permission.

M ost countries accept termination of pregnancy as one acceptable choice when a conceptus (embryo or fetus) is shown to be affected by a serious medical condition, whether inherited or acquired. This practice is explicitly legal in some states in Australia and in most European countries, and is separate in law from any general right of a woman to determine whether a pregnancy can be terminated (as in the United States). There is growing concern, both on the part of "disability activists" and the community, as to whether this practice is unethical because it implies discrimination against those with disability, especially those with the disability that is being tested for.

During a recent meeting on ethics and genetics in Melbourne [Australia], a discussion of prenatal diagnosis (PND) for achondroplasia (a dwarfing condition where there is no intellectual disability, moderate to severe skeletal problems, and mild to moderate social stigma) led to a discussion of alternative technologies. Prenatal diagnosis for achondroplasia, as for most single gene disorders, can be offered to families known to be at risk either by DNA analysis of chorionic villi sampled early in an established pregnancy, or by DNA analysis of one cell from an eight cell embryo (preimplantation genetic diagnosis, or PGD). If the latter method is used, only unaffected embryos are implanted in the womb, and any resulting pregnancy will be unaffected by achondroplasia.

Tests on an embryo or fetus can be carried out at different times, depending on technical resources and the nature of the disorder, including prefertilisation, preimplantation, at l0 to 14 weeks by chorionic villus sampling (CVS), between 10 and 20 weeks by ultrasound and/or maternal serum screening, by amniocentesis at more than 15 weeks, or by x ray. We will consider two of the options available in Melbourne for single gene disorders, DNA testing of an embryo after IVF (following which an embryo that is genetically shown to be unaffected is implanted) or DNA testing by chorionic villus sampling at 10 to 12 weeks (following which an affected fetus can be aborted). These are, in our experience, the major options offered to and considered by couples wishing to avoid the birth of a child with a genetic handicap.

At the Melbourne meeting, the point was made by Dr

Tom Shakespeare, an academic sociologist who has achondroplasia, that he has fewer problems with choice of an embryo unaffected by achondroplasia for implantation after IVF than he does with diagnosis and termination early in pregnancy. This is also the position taken by women who had experienced IVF for infertility reasons or who are at high risk of having an affected embryo due to a single gene disorder. In the recent experience of Genetic Health Services Victoria, couples at one in four risk of having a child with a serious inherited disease will often choose IVF followed by PGD, rather than abortion following CVS.

Both IVF and termination during first trimester are invasive procedures. If "life begins at fertilisation", then IVF and abortion equally involve the "killing" of a fetus (or "allowing embryos to die" which may be viewed as "killing"). Both involve selection against handicap. Why is there an ethical difference in how individuals view PGD as compared to abortion following CVS?

Discriminating Against the Disabled?

The avoidance of the birth of a child who would be affected by a serious disability was one of the justifications for the introduction of access to abortion during the 1970s, when PND first became available. Some disability activists now argue, however, that the use of PND in this way discriminates against people with disabilities for various reasons, including their lives not being valued as equal to those people who do not have a disability. The International Sub-Committee of the British Council of Disabled People, in a statement on "the new genetics", points out that there are far more persons with disability due to environmental causes such as traffic accidents and accidents at work than due to genetic disorders. They argue that free choice can only exist in the context of a society that does not discriminate against individuals with a disability, and that supporting the right of choice for termination requires an equal commitment to supporting the rights of the disabled.

It should be noted, however, that society does not condone or encourage disability in environmental contexts; indeed, society spends significant resources (financial, educational, and otherwise) trying to prevent such accidents from happening. As an example, resources aimed at reducing road accidents, including media campaigns and police resources, are significant. This allocation of resources would not be regarded as discriminatory. It has been equally strongly argued that the decision to terminate an "affected pregnancy" does not make a discriminatory statement against the disabled. . . .

As with abortion, some disability activists believe it is discriminatory to select an embryo that does not have an "affected gene". Other ethicists argue that if an informed choice can be made, the mother (or the parents) has a moral obligation to select an embryo without a disabling gene. It can be argued that given a choice between several possible children, the child to be born should be the one with the chance for the best possible life. [Ethicist Julian] Savulescu states that: "selection for non-disease genes which significantly impact on well-being is morally required." He believes that mothers/parents should be given all available test results followed by non-coercive advice as to which child will have the opportunity of having the best possible life, and argues that it is the parents' decision which embryo to select. . . .

The Moral Status of the Embryo and the Significance of Timing

All human life deserves respect, although in law this respect is reserved for a child after birth; the embryo and fetus have no legal status, at least before viability, in most jurisdictions. This respect is not normally accorded in the same way to human skin or blood cells in culture, or human sperm or eggs prior to fertilisation. While there is no agreement on "when human life begins", key events occur at fertilisation of the egg by the sperm, at implantation of the embryo in the uterus (about eight days), and at the point when a developing nervous system can be detected (about fourteen days). More than half of the total number of embryos (eggs fertilised by sperm) spontaneously abort, however, and pregnancies are not regarded as established clinically until the end of the first trimester (thirteen weeks). Traditionally, most women increase their identification with an embryo as pregnancy progresses, giving full respect to its individuality after quickening (about 15–18 weeks of pregnancy) when they begin to feel fetal movements.

A Moral Choice

On October 25, 1995, I gave birth for the first time, to a boy my husband and I named Henry. Henry was a sweet and precious baby, born with a rare, fatal disease called Fanconi anemia that threatened to take his life before he learned to read, climb a tree or fall in love.

Fanconi anemia (FA) is often accompanied by numerous serious birth defects and always causes bone marrow failure, necessitating a bone marrow transplant. In addition, children with FA are predisposed to cancer. In short, FA is a child killer. . . .

On the day we found out I was pregnant with our second child, Allen and I got a phone call that forever changed our lives. We were informed that there was a fifth option, an experimental procedure that was newly available for FA families—embryo selection using preimplantation genetic diagnosis (PGD). This procedure combines in vitro fertilization (IVF) with genetic testing conducted prior to embryo transfer. Best of all it would allow us to know at the outset of our pregnancy that our baby was healthy and, by using the umbilical cord blood collected at birth, could also be a bone marrow match for Henry. PGD had been used in the past to screen for fatal, childhood diseases like Fanconi anemia, sickle cell anemia and cystic fibrosis, among others, but it had never been used to start a life and save a life at once.

We considered the ethical implications of this procedure, paying close attention to our role and responsibility to protect and advocate for Henry as well as our future children. Allen and I had decided that we couldn't knowingly have another baby with this disease and were therefore very comfortable using PGD to diagnose and transfer only those embryos free of Fanconi anemia. For us, that was the moral thing to do. Not because of what we could or could not endure, but because of what we knew the child must endure throughout his life.

Laurie Goldberg Strongin, "The Promise of Preimplantation Genetic Diagnosis," Genetics & Public Policy Center, www.dnapolicy.org/pdfs/Strongin_PGD_7.03.pdf.

Until recently the pregnant woman had no way to confirm her pregnancy until quickening. With modern ultrasound equipment the fetus can now be monitored almost from conception, and many illnesses and abnormalities can be detected early. The fetus is visualised and is seen as an active individual to be, "a complex responsive organism interacting actively with its intrauterine environment". This is one reason why both pregnant women and health care professionals are more reluctant than previously to offer the option of abortion at later stages of pregnancy. The availability of scanning early in pregnancy results in pregnant women identifying with the embryo and giving it individual moral status earlier. It also puts pressure on women to make an earlier choice on whether to end a pregnancy that will result in disability. This may, in part, explain why women who are at risk of having a child with an inherited genetic disability prefer PGD to CVS.

Once having made a decision to have a child, the woman (or the parents) becomes conscious of time in a number of ways. Initially she is anxious to establish a healthy pregnancy, as soon as possible. This is not always possible, particularly in the context of genetic risk.

When a woman (or couple) is at risk of having a child with a genetic illness, choosing PGD ensures the woman has an embryo unaffected by the genetic illness implanted in her womb from the beginning of the pregnancy. Prenatal genetic diagnosis therefore eliminates the anxiety experienced during the first weeks of a pregnancy established by sexual intercourse, before CVS could be performed, even if the pregnancy is unaffected and proceeds to term.

The Distinction Between PGD and CVS/Abortion

(a) In each case, the intention is to allow the birth of a healthy child. In the case of a dominant disorder such as achondroplasia, one of the parents is affected by the disorder (unless penetrance is highly variable, which is not the case for achondroplasia). Making a choice to terminate an affected pregnancy may be seen as a very personal issue for the affected parent and his/her partner. Termination of pregnancy in the first trimester is usually perceived as a procedure involving the killing of a living fetus in utero.

(b) In most cases where a pregnancy is terminated during

the first trimester because the fetus is affected by a serious inherited disease, the couple conceive again within a year. They continue to conceive (using PND for each pregnancy) until they achieve the number of healthy children desired.

(c) If diagnosis is by CVS at approximately ten weeks, however, followed by termination of an affected pregnancy, there is a temporal difference between the termination and the establishment of a successful unaffected pregnancy. Even if a successful unaffected pregnancy results, as it often does, this occurs later than and independent of the terminated pregnancy. We believe that for many people this would be thought of as "killing".

(d) If diagnosis takes place by embryo biopsy after IVF, several equivalent embryos are tested simultaneously. Some will be affected, some will not. A choice is made to implant some that will give children who are not affected. The others are discarded. The decision to choose an unaffected embryo is made simultaneously with the decision not to choose an affected embryo. There is both a decision to "let live" and a decision to "let die".

(e) When the eight cell embryo is in culture, it has not acquired the additional respect and emotional attachment associated with implantation, growth or ultrasound visualisation. The embryo is still in the charge of a laboratory, and decisions that are taken do not involve the mother in a physical process where she participates in termination of pregnancy. An eight cell embryo can be regarded as a "possible life", similar to an egg and sperm or a human skin cell, while a ten week embryo in utero has more status, perhaps equivalent to a "developing life" with greater realised potential.

Positives Balance Negatives in PGD

We suggest that the major ethical distinction between these two cases is the fact that creating an unaffected and presumably more healthy fetus (and ultimately child) is made simultaneously with the decision to allow the affected embryo to die. In this decision positives balance negatives. This compares with a decision to terminate a ten week embryo following CVS, which can be regarded as "killing" rather than "letting die" and which has no intrinsic balance at the time (although this balance may be restored if there is a later successful unaffected pregnancy).

A second difference relates to the increasing status and attachment that a woman gives to an embryo in utero as it develops, as against an embryo in a laboratory. Although the couple participate in the decision as to how the laboratory staff will treat an unused IVF embryo, the laboratory staff carry out these decisions without direct participation by the woman or her partner. When invasive procedures are performed at 10 to 12 weeks, the woman is intimately involved.

What we find most interesting in this scenario is that the ethical decisions taken are far closer to an ad hoc, relativist, and utilitarian model than one based on any of religious codes, scientific knowledge, consistency in the view of the status of the embryo, or a rigid view of the value of someone with a disability. The ethics of prenatal testing change with the technology available, at least from the point of view of the couple at risk of having a child who will be severely affected.

"*Is it acceptable to undermine the dignity of human life in the name of medical progress?*"

Stem Cell Research Destroys Human Life

Jacqueline Lee

Many scientists believe that embryonic stem cells will prove more useful than adult stem cells in treating diseases because they can develop into any kind of cell and are thus more versatile. But embryonic stem cell research is controversial because it involves discarding embryos once particular cells have been harvested. In the following viewpoint Jacqueline Lee asserts that embryonic stem cell research is unethical because it involves the destruction of human life. Supporters of the research argue that it may lead to cures for genetic diseases and thus reduce human suffering. Lee acknowledges that this is a laudable goal, but she maintains that noble ends must not be achieved through immoral means. She concludes that human embryos should not be destroyed for medical research, no matter what the possible benefits. Lee is a freelance writer.

As you read, consider the following questions:

1. What other type of stem cell does the author suggest can be used for medical research?
2. What three principles of the Nuremberg Code does embryonic stem cell research violate, in Lee's opinion?

Watching someone you love turn to stone before your eyes can definitely affect your perspective on the embryonic stem-cell research debate. In 1999, my mother was diagnosed with scleroderma, which literally means hard skin. For a person with this rare disease, the immune system, which is supposed to attack the pathogens that make us ill, turns instead on healthy body tissues. Symptoms may begin with tightening and thickening of the skin along with joint and muscle pain. Patients may then develop Raynaud's phenomenon, a condition in which the body's extremities change color in response to temperature. Others may develop calcinosis, white lumps beneath the skin that can erupt, leaving painful ulcers.

My mother's first symptom was shortness of breath. The disease viciously attacked her lungs and other internal organs, and she died of respiratory failure within seven months of her diagnosis. During that time, she lost the ability to get up from a sitting position without assistance. She lost 50 pounds because she could not eat anything without vomiting. She lost her ability to breathe. In the end, instead of praying for her recovery, I began to pray that she would be released from her struggle with the disease. As soon as she died, I begged God for the chance to take that prayer back.

The Arguments for Stem-Cell Research

According to research presented [in 2001] by University of Florida professor of medicine John R. Wingard, stem-cell transplants show remarkable promise in treating not only scleroderma but also other autoimmune diseases like multiple sclerosis and lupus. Essentially, stem cells are the body's "master cells." They can differentiate into other types of cells, from brain cells to skin cells. Feasibly, stem cells might be injected into the nervous system to replace tissues damaged by strokes, Alzheimer's, Parkinson's, or spinal cord injuries.

I am excited about the potential of stem-cell therapies, but recent demands that the federal government fund research on embryonic stem cells frighten me. Extracting stem cells from embryos proves contentious, of course, because embryos must be destroyed in order to obtain the cells.

Supporters of embryonic stem-cell research cite two main

advantages of embryonic stem cells—both of them, ultimately, economic. According to the National Institutes of Health, stem cells from embryos, so-called "pluripotent" cells, are more flexible than adult stem cells and can thus be manipulated into more types of body tissues, including bone, skin, and muscle. Those who support federal funding of embryonic stem-cell research claim that pluripotent cells are more useful than adult stem cells because they possess these remarkable powers of transformation. In addition, scientists can generate an unlimited number of embryonic stem cells in the laboratory. Because adult cells are more difficult to obtain, embryos would be a more cost-effective source of cells.

"We are now witnessing the gradual restructuring of American culture according to ideals of utility, productivity, and cost-effectiveness," wrote the U.S. Catholic bishops in Living the Gospel of Life: A Challenge to American Catholics. "It is a culture where moral questions are submerged by a river of goods and services."

The Potential of Adult Stem-Cell Research

But opponents of embryonic research, ironically, are able to cite the economic argument, too. According to [an] article by Scott Gottlieb in the *American Spectator*, investors of venture capital currently fund adult stem-cell research much more frequently than they fund embryonic research. Why? Embryonic cells have never been used in humans, but adult cells have.

Opponents also note that embryonic cells can, at times, be too flexible. Gottlieb notes that the injection of pluripotent cells in mice, for instance, has caused the growth of tumors consisting of numerous body tissue types; the cells did not integrate themselves into damaged tissues as scientists hoped they would. Also, conceivably, a transplanted embryonic stem cell could be rejected by the recipient's body—much like the body tries to reject a transplanted organ. Adult stem cells, however, are more specialized and, because adult stem cells are harvested from the patient's own body, rejection is not a factor.

Apart from medical and economic arguments, we as Catholics must wade through the ambiguous moral arguments both for and against embryonic research. While many prolife Catholic organizations, including the National Catholic Bioethics Center, have staunchly opposed stem-cell research, according to a *Wall Street Journal*/NBC News Poll, a majority of Catholics surveyed—72 percent—support it.

A New Watershed

The humanity of the human embryo is not a religious question, but a matter of empirical fact. What is at stake at present is the production of tiny human lives for reasons entirely unrelated to the good of those lives. A new watershed is about to be crossed in our nation no less momentous than the one crossed in 1973 when the Supreme Court invented the constitutional right of abortion. And given the fact that there are morally acceptable alternative sources for stem cells—for example, stem cells found in adult bone marrow, adipose tissue, fetal umbilical cords and placenta, which, according to the latest research, promise equal if not greater results than embryonic stem cells—the question of proceeding with the making and destroying of human embryos should not even be an issue. After the grave mistakes and horrors of the past century, shouldn't we resist the temptation to watch silently while an entire class of human beings, in this case embryonic human life, is resigned to a moral status no higher than a laboratory rat?

E. Christian Brugger, *New Oxford Review*, October 2003.

Senator Orrin Hatch of Utah, a leading supporter of embryonic research, argues that "a frozen embryo in a refrigerator in a clinic" is not the same as "a fetus developing in a mother's womb." These frozen embryos, his supporters say, have the potential to develop into life—but the embryos themselves are not technically alive.

Many bioethicists, however, dismiss that argument as pointless rationalization. If all humans begin as embryos, how can embryos not be considered "alive"? Furthermore, if these embryos are alive, then extracting embryonic stem cells violates at least three principles of the Nuremberg Code, which lays out principles scientists must observe when conducting research on human subjects. First, scientists must always obtain the voluntary consent of every human research subject. Embryos, of course, cannot give their consent. Also, when scientists create embryos specifically for the purposes of experimentation, the embryos do not even have parents who can speak on their behalf. Second, the Nuremberg Code states that human subjects should be protected "against even remote possibilities of injury, disability, or death." Third, the Nuremberg Code requires that experiments on human subjects must yield results "unprocurable by any other means of study."

If experimental treatments involving adult cells have already furnished promising results, why do we need embryonic cells? And if embryonic research violates the codes we have established to protect human dignity, how can we, as moral people, even consider carrying it out?

As Tommy Thompson, U.S. Secretary of Health and Human Services—and a prominent Catholic—observes, "There is nothing easy about this issue. It balances our respect for human life with our highest hopes for alleviating human suffering." True, pluripotent cells in and of themselves cannot develop into human beings. However, scientists cannot obtain pluripotent cells without destroying the four-day-old embryos from which they come. "As long as embryos are destroyed as part of the research enterprise," says the National Bioethics Advisory Council, "researchers using embryonic stem cells (and those who fund them) will be complicit in the death of embryos."

With his decision in August [2001], President [George W.] Bush has already authorized limited funding for research on existing stem-cell lines. . . . Although many respect Bush's compromise, my own fear is that his willingness to allow a little funding has paved the way for steady relaxation of current restrictions.

The Ends Cannot Justify the Means

Ultimately, it comes down to this: can we really justify the willful destruction of human embryos by arguing that "the end justifies the means"? Is it acceptable to undermine the dignity of human life in the name of medical progress?

Perhaps many of us are looking at this issue through swollen eyes blurred by tears. We have all seen the suffering brought on by degenerative illness, either in ourselves or in someone we love. Our hearts ache for those who suffer, and we want to do anything by any means to stop it.

But, no matter how laudable that aim may be, it cannot justify the destruction of a developing human life. In the words of Charlotte Bronte's Jane Eyre, "Law and principles are not for times when there is no temptation: They are for such moments as this, when body and soul rise in mutiny against their rigor. If at my individual convenience I might break them, what would be their worth?"

My heart ached for my mother, and today it aches for all those who suffer from disease and injury; but, no matter how deep my desire to ease that suffering may be, it cannot justify the destruction of a developing human life. I wish that my mother had been strong enough to undergo a stem-cell transplant. I would have done anything to save her.

Well, almost anything. I would not have been complicit in the destruction of human life, even if the destruction of that life could have saved hers. To me, a praiseworthy end could never have justified such a destructive means.

> *"Stem cells are a unique medical and scientific resource."*

Stem Cell Research Can Save Lives

NARAL Pro-Choice America

NARAL Pro-Choice America is a national advocacy organization that promotes personal privacy and a woman's right to choose. In the following viewpoint NARAL criticizes President George W. Bush's limits on federal funding for embryonic stem cell research. Such research has the potential to cure many devastating diseases, the authors write. According to NARAL, stem cells do not have the capacity to develop into a full human being, and the stem cells used in the research are taken from excess embryos created in fertility treatments—embryos that would have been destroyed anyway. NARAL asserts that Bush's policy of requiring federally funded researchers to use only stem cell lines created before August 9, 2001, was enacted solely to appease antichoice groups.

As you read, consider the following questions:

1. What are some of the diseases that embryonic stem cell research could cure, according to NARAL?
2. Why, in NARAL's view, do many in the antichoice movement oppose stem cell research?
3. Concerns about the adequacy of stem cell lines available under the Bush restrictions center on what five issues, as listed by the organization?

NARAL Pro-Choice America, "Bush Administration Stem Cell Policy Hamstrings Vital Health Research," www.ProchoiceAmerica.org, January 1, 2004. Copyright © 2004 by NARAL.org. Reproduced by permission.

S tem cell research promises significant medical advances. It may lead to treatment for diseases and disabilities such as Parkinson's and Alzheimer's, spinal cord injury, stroke, burns, heart disease, diabetes, osteoarthritis and rheumatoid arthritis. The possibilities are endless. However, President [George W.] Bush and anti-choice forces have placed nearly impossible constraints on this vital research. President Bush has decided that the federal government may only conduct or fund research on stem cell lines derived before the arbitrary date of August 9, 2001. This policy is both ethically incoherent and seriously damaging to this critical medical research. The existing stem cell lines simply are not sufficient to allow researchers to develop the cures that are expected from this endeavor. Thus, time is running out for millions of disease sufferers, and much research that would otherwise be undertaken in the public sector will be forced into the private realm, where it will not receive the benefit of the strict ethical scrutiny and oversight that comes with public funding.

The Promise of Stem Cell Research

Stem cells are cells that can develop into almost any type of cell. There are both *embryonic* stem cells and *adult* stem cells. The controversy surrounding stem cell research and President Bush's policy concern only embryonic stem cells. Research using adult stem cells is not controversial, but adult stem cell research is not an adequate substitute for embryonic stem cell research. Embryonic stem cells have the greatest potential to create cures for a number of diseases, as they have the ability to become the widest range of cells. (This is known as "pluripotency.") While adult stem cells also show promise for certain diseases, such as liver disease and multiple sclerosis, some studies have shown they are less likely to be useful in many other areas, such as diabetes or diseases of the brain and nervous system. The National Institutes of Health (NIH) has stressed the importance of pursuing research with both embryonic and adult stem cells.

In embryonic stem cell research, a cluster of cells is isolated from an embryo that was created in the laboratory through in vitro fertilization. These embryos were generally created as part of fertility treatments, but are no longer needed and would otherwise be discarded. The stem cells then are allowed to regenerate into a "line" of cells that have the potential to create healthy new cells that may be able to replace tissue that has been damaged by disease or injury. Stem cells do not have the capacity to develop into a full human being.

Stem cells are a unique medical and scientific resource. Scientists at respected medical and educational institutions, from the members of the National Bioethics Advisory Committee (NBAC) to the over 9,000 members of the American Society for Cell Biology to the National Academy of Sciences, anticipate that stem cell research may lead to significant advances in medical science, including the following:

- Tissue transplantation, to replace damaged or diseased tissue, such as heart tissue following a heart attack.
- Generation of neurons to cure Parkinson's disease.
- Growth of cartilage-forming cells to alleviate arthritis.
- Research into curing diseases such as cancer, birth defects, and diabetes.
- Drug research and testing, allowing the testing of the safety and efficacy of drugs directly against human tissues, rather than relying on animal models for research.

The History of Federal Funding for Stem Cell Research

Since 1996, federal law has banned federal funding of human embryo research. However, in January 1999 the Department of Health and Human Services (HHS) concluded that the congressional ban on funding research using human embryos did not extend to stem cell research, since stem cells are not embryos and do not have the potential to develop into a fetus or a person. Following extensive public discussions involving scientists, doctors, patients, lawyers, and ethicists, the NIH issued guidelines for federally funded stem cell research. The guidelines established limits on stem cell research funding; for instance, federal funding could not have been used to *derive* stem cells from embryos; it could only have been used for research involving stem cells that were derived using private funds. The stem cells could only have been derived from frozen embryos that were created for fertility treatment and were in excess of those needed for the treatment. The guidelines also included thorough informed consent requirements for the donors, ensured that there was a clear separation between the fertility treatment and decision to donate, and ensured that the donors could expect no direct benefit from the decision to donate.

During the 2000 campaign, then-Governor George Bush indicated he would review and probably reverse the Clinton administration's policies on stem cell research. He had "consistently opposed federal funding for research that requires embryos to be discarded or destroyed," his spokesman said. The review of the guidelines engendered extensive public debate and controversy. Many in the anti-choice movement oppose stem cell research because they wish to ascribe to every fertilized egg in a petri dish the moral and legal status of a person. This position, however, is impossible to reconcile with well-accepted practices of in vitro fertilization and contraception. In vitro fertilization typically requires the creation and transfer to the uterus of many embryos for every live birth. Embryos are also commonly discarded after a successful pregnancy or when a couple decides not to continue to attempt to get pregnant. In the case of contraception, several common forms (the pill and the intra-uterine device (IUD), for example), as well as emergency contraception, work, among other ways, by preventing a fertilized egg from implanting in the uterine wall.

On the other side of the debate are the scientists, clinicians, patients, and their families who hope to be able to take full advantage of this promising new technology. Many in the religious community strongly support the research. Over 80 Nobel laureates wrote to President Bush arguing against regulations that would limit research to those stem cells derived from adult tissues. Patient advocacy groups ranging from the American Diabetes Association to the Parkinson's Action Network support stem cell research. Even a number of anti-choice politicians support stem cell research.

The Bush Compromise: Politically Expedient, Morally Incoherent

Caught between an American public that strongly supports federally funded stem cell research and an anti-choice constituency demanding that no research go forward, President Bush sought a way out. In trying to find a middle ground, the Administration developed a politically expedient but morally incoherent policy. The new policy allows federal funding for stem cell research only for research on existing stem cell lines that were derived: (1) with the informed consent of the donors; (2) from the excess embryos created solely for reproductive purposes; (3) without any financial inducements to the donors; and (4) that the derivation process must have been initiated prior to 9:00 p.m. EDT on August 9, 2001.

O'Farrell. © 2004 by Cagle Cartoons. Reproduced by permission.

The key point to the President's policy is that it refuses to allow any stem cell lines created after an arbitrary date. However, it fails to justify why research conducted before this date is acceptable, while research conducted after this date is not. According to Arthur Caplan, head of the Center for Bioethics at the University of Pennsylvania, "The problem with the president's policy is that it is hopelessly arbitrary and illogical. Why is it ethical to use stem cells made from human embryos before August 9, 2001, but not after?"

The Inadequacy of Preexisting Stem Cell Lines

Aside from its moral incoherency, the new policy has a number of practical limitations, most of which relate to the adequacy of the cell lines derived before the policy's arbitrary deadline. The National Institutes of Health initially identified 78 cell lines worldwide that were derived in accordance with the Administration's new policy. However, the NIH has acknowledged that "[t]here are serious issues about when the cells will be practically available." Currently, NIH lists just nine (9) stem cell lines available to researchers on its registry.

Concerns about the adequacy of stem cell lines available under the Bush restrictions center on (1) quality; (2) longevity; (3) genetic diversity; (4) ownership; and (5) compliance with ethical standards.

1. *Quality.* Little is known about the quality or viability of the cell lines in the NIH registry. Each stem cell line is unique and will differ in many characteristics, including its ability to generate into other types of cell lines. Perhaps of greatest concern, many existing cell lines were cultured with animal cells or serum, which could pose health risks if used in humans. However, newer methods allow stem cells to be cultivated with other human cells, avoiding the chance of contamination with animal viruses.

2. *Longevity.* Although stem cell lines are sometimes referred to as being "immortal" most scientists expect that they will in fact degrade over time. Thus, replacement cell lines will need to be derived from time to time if any meaningful research is to be undertaken.

3. *Genetic Diversity.* Many researchers are concerned about the lack of genetic diversity among existing lines. The great majority of the stem cells on the NIH registry appear to have been derived from white couples, meaning they may be of limited use to non-Europeans. If stem cells are to be used to treat injury and disease, the tissues and cells that are produced must be injected into the body. As with blood transfusions or organ transplants, these cells must "match" the patient to minimize the extent to which the patient's body rejects the foreign tissue. Harold Varmus, former head of the

National Institutes of Health and current director of Memorial Sloan-Kettering Cancer Center, and Douglas Melton, leading Harvard cell biologist, have cautioned that "even 100 good lines will likely be inadequate to treat our genetically diverse population without encountering immune rejection."

4. *Ownership.* All the cell lines on the NIH registry were derived with private funds and/or in foreign nations. The availability of these cell lines to U.S. researchers, and the rights to any products that are derived from the lines, are very much in the doubt. For example, obtaining living material from foreign sources requires "material transfer agreements," which can take months or even years to execute.

5. *Ethical Considerations.* The Bush ethical guidelines are weaker than both those under the Clinton policy and those required by many universities and other research institutions. Thus, some of the cell lines on the NIH register may not be available to many U.S. researchers if they don't meet the ethical guidelines required by the researcher's home institution. The NIH has acknowledged that it did not study the adequacy of the informed consent forms completed by donors, but that the standard would be whatever was in place in the country or facility where the work was performed. The American Association for the Advancement of Science has noted that "[t]oo often we have learned that procedures used in other parts of the world in research with human subjects do not measure up to the ethical standards we embrace in this country."

These concerns have prompted a renewed debate about the president's stem cell policy. In April 2003 Senator Arlen Specter (R-PA) asked the Bush administration to allow for more human cell stem lines to be generated after confirming a potential supply of safer stem cells that were not grown on mouse cells. In November 2003 a medical ethics panel, comprised of scientists, philosophers, ethicists and lawyers, met at Johns Hopkins University and echoed the same sentiments. According to the panel, treating patients with the embryonic stem cells approved by President Bush for federal funding would be "unethical and risky." There are safer stem cells that exist and are currently being used around the world, but the administration refuses to make them eligible for federal funding.

The United States is the worldwide leader in biomedical research, but with ever-tightening politically motivated restrictions, its future position remains uncertain. At least one leading scientist, Roger Pedersen, formerly of the University of California, San Francisco, has left the United States for the University of Cambridge where he can pursue his work under the more rational British regulations. Jeffrey Kahn, director of the Center for Bioethics, believes that Dr. Pedersen is only the first in what will become a "brain drain" as American scientists relocate in order to pursue their research away from what many see as "overly puritanical restrictions from Washington."

Paul Berg, Cahill Professor of Cancer Research at Stanford University and Nobel laureate, worried the United States is losing ground: "I'm absolutely amazed at how little has been accomplished . . . following the president's announcement. . . . If you look at what's happening elsewhere, in Australia, Israel and England . . . they are rushing into this area of science because they see its promise. But here there's just no evidence of urgency." Keith Yamamoto, vice dean for research at the University of California, echoed Dr. Berg's concerns stating, "Normally . . . many young people would be diving into this field. . . . It's clear to me there's been a chilling effect." Actor Christopher Reeve, who suffered a paralyzing spinal-cord injury in a horse-riding accident, gives a poignant perspective: "It is painful to contemplate where we might be today if embryonic stem cell research had been allowed to go forward with full support of the government.'"

The federal government plays the most critical role in developing new biomedical technologies. Because marketable products from stem cell research are still years away, the private sector simply will not make the level of investment that is needed if we are to see the treatments and cures that this technology promises. Furthermore, government funding ensures appropriate oversight and public scrutiny of research. The limited and weak compromise on federal funding for stem cell research holds the health—indeed, the lives—of millions of Americans hostage.

Periodical Bibliography

The following articles have been selected to supplement the diverse views presented in this chapter.

Nell Boyce	"A Law's Fetal Flaw," *U.S. News & World Report*, July 21, 2003.
Shelley Burtt	"Which Babies?" *Tikkun*, January 2001.
Commonweal	"Grass-Roots Eugenics," July 16, 2004.
John Gillott	"Screening for Disability: A Eugenic Pursuit?" *Journal of Medical Ethics*, October 2001.
Fred Guterl	"To Build a Baby," *Newsweek*, June 30, 2003.
Amy Laura Hall	"Price to Pay: The Misuse of Embryos," *Christian Century*, June 1, 2004.
Agnes R. Howard	"Building a Better Baby: The Dark Side of Universal Prenatal Screening," *Weekly Standard*, April 5, 2004.
Jill Joynt and Vasugi Ganeshananthan	"Abortion Decisions," *Atlantic Monthly*, April 2003.
Michael Kinsley	"The False Controversy of Stem Cells," *Time*, May 31, 2004.
Michael Kinsley	"Life Altering," *New Republic*, November 1, 2004.
Paul Lauritzen	"Neither Person nor Property: Embryo Research and the Status of the Early Embryo," *America*, March 26, 2001.
Newsweek	"Stem Cell Division," October 25, 2004.
Rammesh Ponnoru	"Cells, Fetuses, and Logic," *Human Life Review*, Summer 2001.
Rita Rubin	"Early Genetic Testing Allays Fears, Ignites Ethics Debate," *USA Today*, May 26, 2004.
Sacha Zimmerman	"Fetal Position," *New Republic*, August 18, 2003.

For Further Discussion

Chapter 1

1. William P. Saunders believes that abortion destroys human life, while Caitlin Borgmann and Catherine Weiss argue that prohibitions on abortion subjugate women. Whose viewpoint do you find most convincing, and why?

2. Jon Daugherty, Leonard Peikoff, and Gregg Easterbrook offer three different views on when human personhood begins. Which comes closest to your own view on this issue? Explain your answer.

3. Karen Houppert argues that the central issue in the abortion debate is not when personhood begins, but whether it is moral to prohibit a woman from controlling her body. Based on the viewpoints in the chapter, do you feel that the government should restrict or prohibit abortion? Why or why not?

Chapter 2

1. What evidence do Felicia H. Stewart and Philip D. Darney offer to support their view that legal abortion benefits women? What evidence does Candace C. Crandall offer to show that abortion has harmed women? Whose viewpoint is more persuasive, and why?

2. Ian Gentles argues that abortion is dangerous, while the viewpoint by NARAL Pro-Choice America emphasizes that banning abortion results in more danger for women. How does each viewpoint influence your opinion on the legality of abortion?

3. Valerie Meehan argues that abortion harms women emotionally. How does Noy Thrupkaew rebut this claim? What points in each viewpoint do you find most persuasive?

Chapter 3

1. How does Rachel Benson Gold describe the plight of women seeking abortion before *Roe v. Wade*? What parts of this picture does Raymond J. Adamek take issue with? Does either viewpoint influence your opinion on the legality of abortion, and if so, how?

2. Hanes Swingle describes a late-term abortion in great detail, while Simon Heller addresses the constitutionality of the 2003 Partial Birth Abortion Ban Act. Whose rhetorical approach do you find most persuasive, and why?

3. Do you feel that the United States' "Mexico City" policy, as described by Marty Meehan, Gloria Feldt, and Gail Quinn, is a good one? Explain your answer.

Chapter 4

1. After reading the viewpoints by John F. Kilner, C. Cameron, and R. Williamson, do you feel that using genetic testing to screen for genetic disease discriminates against the disabled? Explain your answer.

2. After reading the viewpoints by John F. Kilner, C. Cameron, and R. Williamson, do you feel that preimplantation genetic diagnosis is more ethically acceptable than abortion? Explain your answer.

3. Do you agree more with Jacqueline Lee's or NARAL Pro-Choice America's view on embryonic stem cell research? How is your view on abortion related to your opinion of embryonic stem cell research?

Organizations to Contact

The editors have compiled the following list of organizations concerned with the issues debated in this book. The descriptions are derived from materials provided by the organizations. All have publications or information available for interested readers. The list was compiled on the date of publication of the present volume; the information provided here may change. Be aware that many organizations take several weeks or longer to respond to inquiries, so allow as much time as possible.

ACLU Reproductive Freedom Project
125 Broad St., Eighteenth Floor, New York, NY 10004
(212) 549-2633 • fax: (212) 549-2652
e-mail: RFP@aclu.org • Web site: www.aclu.org

A branch of the American Civil Liberties Union, the project coordinates efforts in litigation, advocacy, and public education to guarantee the constitutional right to reproductive choice. Its mission is to ensure that reproductive decisions will be informed, meaningful, and free of hindrance or coercion from the government. The project disseminates position papers, fact sheets, legislative documents, and publications including *Abortion Bans: Myths and Facts* and *The ACLU Opposes Federal Restrictions on Mifepristone (RU-486)*.

Advocates for Youth
2000 M St. NW, Washington, DC 20036
(202) 419-3420 • fax: (202) 419-1448
e-mail: questions@advocatesforyouth.org
Web site: www.advocatesforyouth.org

Advocates for Youth is dedicated to creating programs and advocating for policies that help young people make informed and responsible decisions about their reproductive and sexual health. It provides information, education, and advocacy to youth-serving agencies and professionals, policy makers, and the media. Among the organization's numerous publications are the fact sheets "Adolescents and Abortion," and "Peer Education: Promoting Healthy Behaviors."

Alan Guttmacher Institute (AGI)
120 Wall St., Twenty-first Floor, New York, NY 10005
(212) 248-1111 • fax: (212) 248-1951
e-mail: info@guttmacher.org • Web site: www.agi-usa.org

The institute is a reproduction research group that advocates the right to safe and legal abortion. It provides extensive statistical information on abortion and voluntary population control. Its publications include *Perspectives on Sexual and Reproductive Health* and *International Family Planning Perspectives*.

American Life League (ALL)
PO Box 1350, Stafford, VA 22555
(540) 659-4171 • fax: (540) 659-2586
e-mail: office@all.org • Web site: www.all.org

ALL promotes family values and opposes abortion. The organization monitors congressional activities dealing with pro-life issues and provides information on the physical and psychological risks of abortion. It produces educational materials, books, flyers, and programs for pro-family organizations that oppose abortion. The league's publications include the bimonthly magazine *Celebrate Life* and the monthly *Pro-Life Bulletin Board*.

Americans United for Life (AUL)
310 S. Peoria St., Suite 300, Chicago, IL 60607-3534
(312) 492-7234 • fax: (312) 492-7235
e-mail: info@aul.org • Web site: www.unitedforlife.org

AUL promotes legislation to make abortion illegal. The organization operates a library and a legal resource center for such subjects as abortion, infanticide, destructive embryo research, and human cloning. Publications include the articles "Embryo Adoption or Embryo Donation? The Distinction and Its Implications," and "An Authentic Concept of Woman Will Build a Culture of Life."

Catholics for a Free Choice (CFFC)
1436 U St. NW, Suite 301, Washington, DC 20009-3997
(202) 986-6093 • fax: (202) 332-7995
e-mail: cffc@catholicsforchoice.org
Web site: www.cath4choice.org

CFFC supports the right to legal abortion and promotes family planning to reduce the incidents of abortion and to increase women's choice in childbearing and child rearing. It publishes the bimonthly newsletter *Conscience*.

Center for Bio-Ethical Reform (CBR)
PO Box 2339, Santa Fe Springs, CA 90670
(562) 777-9117
e-mail: cbr@cbrinfo.org • Web site: www.cbrinfo.org

CBR opposes legal abortion, focusing its arguments on abortion's moral aspects. Its members frequently address conservative and Christian groups throughout the United States. The center also offers training seminars on fund-raising to pro-life volunteers. CBR's audiotapes include "Harder Truth" and "Abortion and the Hereafter." The center's Genocide Awareness Project (GAP) is a traveling photo-mural exhibit that visits university campuses around the country to make students aware of the broader aspects of abortion.

Center for Reproductive Rights

120 Wall St., New York, NY 10005
(917) 637-3600 • fax: (917) 637-3666
e-mail: info@reprorights.org • Web site: www.crlp.org

The center is a nonprofit legal advocacy organization dedicated to promoting and defending women's reproductive rights worldwide. The center advocates for safe and affordable contraception as well as safe and legal abortion for women. Among the center's publications are fact sheets, briefing papers, and articles, including "What If *Roe* Fell?" and *The Women of the World: Laws and Policies Affecting Their Reproductive Lives.*

Childbirth by Choice Trust

344 Bloor St. West, Suite 502, Toronto, ON M5S 3A7 Canada
(416) 961-7812 • fax: (416) 961-5771
e-mail: info@cbctrust.com • Web site: www.cbctrust.com

Childbirth by Choice Trust's goal is to educate the public about abortion and reproductive choice. It produces educational materials that aim to provide factual, rational, and straightforward information about fertility control issues. The organization's publications include the booklet *Abortion in Law, History, and Religion* and the pamphlets *Unsure About Your Pregnancy? A Guide to Making the Right Decision* and *Information for Teens About Abortion.*

Feminists for Life of America

733 Fifteenth St. NW, Suite 1100, Washington, DC 20005
(202) 737-3352
e-mail: info@feministsforlife.org
Web site: www.feministsforlife.org

This organization is comprised of feminists united to secure the right to life, from conception to natural death, for all human beings. It believes that legal abortion exploits women. The group supports a Human Life Amendment, which would protect unborn life. It promotes an education campaign titled "Women Deserve Better," which promotes women-centered solutions to reduce abortion and protect women's health, and publishes the *American Feminist* magazine.

NARAL Pro-Choice America
1156 Fifteenth St. NW, Suite 700, Washington, DC 20005
(202) 973-3000 • fax: (202) 973-3096
e-mail: naral@naral.org • Web site: www.naral.org

NARAL Pro-Choice America works to develop and sustain a pro-choice political constituency in order to maintain the right of all women to legal abortion. The league briefs members of Congress and testifies at hearings on abortion and related issues. Its publications include "Who Decides: A Reproductive Rights Issues Manual," and "Talking About Freedom of Choice."

National Right to Life Committee (NRLC)
512 Tenth St. NW, Washington, DC 20004
(202) 626-8800
e-mail: nrlc@nrlc.org • Web site: www.nrlc.org

NRLC is one of the largest organizations opposing abortion. The committee campaigns against legislation to legalize abortion. It encourages ratification of a constitutional amendment granting embryos and fetuses the same right to life as living persons, and it advocates alternatives to abortion, such as adoption. NRLC publishes the brochure *When Does Life Begin?* and *Abortion: Some Medical Facts.*

Ontario Consultants on Religious Tolerance (OCRT)
PO Box 128, Watertown, NY 13601-0128
fax: (613) 547-9015
Web site: www.religioustolerance.org

The Ontario Consultants on Religious Tolerance is a group that advocates freedom of religion and firmly supports the separation of church and state. Its purpose is to disseminate accurate religious information and expose religious fraud. The group publishes many essays and articles on "hot topics" including "Abortion: All Sides of the Issue," and "The Key Question: When Does Human Personhood Start?"

Planned Parenthood Federation of America (PPFA)
434 West Thirty-third St., New York, NY 10001
(212) 541-7800 • fax: (212) 245-1845
e-mail: communications@ppfa.org
Web site: www.plannedparenthood.org

PPFA is a national organization that supports people's right to make their own reproductive decisions without governmental interference. It provides contraception, abortion, and family planning services at clinics located throughout the United States. Among its extensive publications are the fact sheets "Abortion After the First Trimester" and "The Emotional Effects of Induced Abortion."

Religious Coalition for Reproductive Choice (RCRC)
1025 Vermont Ave. NW, Suite 1130, Washington, DC 20005
(202) 628-7700 • fax: (202) 628-7716
e-mail: info@rcrc.org • Web site: www.rcrc.org

RCRC consists of more than thirty Christian, Jewish, and other religious groups committed to helping individuals to make decisions concerning abortion in accordance with their consciences. The organization supports abortion rights, opposes antiabortion violence, and educates policy makers and the public about the diversity of religious perspectives on abortion. RCRC publishes booklets, an educational essay series, the quarterly *Faith & Choices* newsletter, the *Speak Out* series including "Just Say Know!" and "Family Planning: A Moral Good, a Human Right."

United States Conference of Catholic Bishops
3211 Fourth St. NE, Washington, DC 20017-1194
(202) 541-3000 • fax: (202) 541-3054
e-mail: pro-life@usccb.org • Web site: www.nccbuscc.org

The United States Conference of Catholic Bishops, which adheres to the Vatican's opposition to abortion, is the American Roman Catholic bishops' organ for unified action. Through its committee on pro-life activities, it advocates a legislative ban on abortion and promotes state restrictions on abortion, such as parental consent/notification laws and strict licensing laws for abortion clinics. Its pro-life publications include the bulletin "Stem Cell Research and Human Cloning," and the brochure "A People of Life."

Bibliography of Books

Randy Alcorn — *ProLife Answers to ProChoice Arguments.* Sisters, OR: Multnomah, 2000.

Hardley Arkes — *Natural Rights and the Right to Choose.* New York: Cambridge University Press, 2002.

Patricia Baird and Eleanor J. Bader — *Targets of Hatred: Anti-Abortion Terrorism.* New York: Palgrave, 2001.

Robert M. Baird and Stuart E. Robinson — *The Ethics of Abortion.* New York: Prometheus Books, 2001.

Linda J. Beckman and S. Marie Harvey, eds. — *The New Civil War: The Psychology, Culture, and Politics of Abortion.* Washington, DC: American Psychological Association, 1998.

Belinda Bennett, ed. — *Abortion.* Burlington, VT: Ashgate, 2004.

Angela Bonoavoglia, ed. — *The Choices We Made: 25 Women and Men Speak Out About Abortion.* New York: Four Walls Eight Windows, 2001.

Theresa Burke — *Forbidden Grief: The Unspoken Pain of Abortion.* Springfield, IL: Acorn Books, 2002.

Guy Condon — *Fatherhood Aborted.* Carol Stream, IL: Tyndale House, 2001.

Gloria Feldt — *Behind Every Choice Is a Story.* Denton: University of North Texas Press, 2004.

Gloria Feldt, with Laura Fraser — *The War on Choice: The Right-Wing Attack on Women's Rights and How to Fight Back.* New York: Bantam, 2004.

David J. Garrow — *Liberty and Sexuality: The Right to Privacy and the Making of Roe v. Wade.* Berkeley: University of California Press, 1998.

N.E.H. Hull and Peter Charles Hoffer — Roe v Wade: *The Abortion Rights Controversy in American History.* Lawrence: University Press of Kansas, 2001.

Krista Jacob — *Our Choices, Our Lives: Unapologetic Writings on Abortion.* Lincoln, NE: iUniverse, 2004.

Leon R. Kass — *Life, Liberty, and the Defense of Dignity: The Challenge of Bioethics.* San Francisco: Encounter Books, 2002.

Scott Klusendorf — *Pro-Life 101: A Step-by-Step Guide to Making Your Case Persuasively.* Signal Hill, CA: Stand to Reason Press, 2002.

Peter Kreeft — *Three Approaches to Abortion: A Thoughtful and Compassionate Guide to Today's Most Controversial Issue.* San Francisco: Ignatius Press, 2002.

Jane Maienschein   *Whose View of Life? Embryos, Cloning, and Stem Cells.* Cambridge, MA: Harvard University Press, 2003.

Carol Mason   *Killing for Life: The Apocalyptic Narrative of Pro-Life Politics.* Ithaca, NY: Cornell University Press, 2002.

Carol J.C. Maxwell   *Pro-Life Activists in America: Meaning, Motivation, and Direct Action.* New York: Cambridge University Press, 2002.

Deborah R. McFarlane and Kenneth J. Meier   *The Politics of Fertility Control: Family Planning and Abortion Policies in the American States.* New York: Chatham House, 2001.

Jeff McMahan   *The Ethics of Killing: Killing at the Margins of Life.* New York: Oxford University Press, 2002.

Erik Parens and Adrienne Asch   *Prenatal Testing and Disability Rights.* Washington, DC: Georgetown University Press, 2000.

James Risen and Judy L. Thomas   *Wrath of Angels: The American Abortion Wars.* New York: Basic Books, 1998.

Anna Runkle   *In Good Conscience: A Practical, Emotional, and Spiritual Guide to Deciding Whether to Have an Abortion.* San Francisco: Anna Runkle, 2002.

William Saletan   *Bearing Right: How Conservatives Won the Abortion War.* Berkeley: University of California Press, 2003.

Alexander Sanger   *Beyond Choice: Reproductive Freedom in the 21st Century.* New York: Public Affairs, 2004.

Rickie Solinger, ed.   *Abortion Wars: A Half Century of Struggle, 1950–2000.* Berkeley: University of California Press, 1998.

Andrea Tone, ed.   *Controlling Reproduction: An American History.* Wilmington, DE: SR Books, 1997.

Teresa R. Wagner, ed.   *Back to the Drawing Board: The Future of the Pro-Life Movement.* South Bend, IN: St. Augustine's Press, 2003.

Index